ROY BENTL
STATIONAR\

Roger Titford

The strange story of how Reading
stood still in the Swinging Sixties

Further Thought Publishing, Inkpen, 2018
www.furtherthought.co.uk

First published in Great Britain 2018 by Further Thought Publishing.
© Roger Titford 2018
The moral right of the author has been asserted.

ISBN 978-0-951-8771-9-7

British Library Cataloguing in Publication Data – A catalogue record for this book is available from the British Library.

To local newspapers, reporters and photographers
without whom we will all be poorer.

Acknowledgements

During the course of writing this book there are many people who deserved to be acknowledged for their part. I hope I have remembered them all but apologies to those I have omitted. Of course, whatever errors there are I must claim.

In particular I would like to mention David Downs and Chris Lee for their continued support, advice and material. I have also received such advice, material and photographs from many other members of the football communities of Reading including Mark Bradley, Roger Ware, Alan Sedunary, Mick Foster, Nigel Meek, Haydn Middleton, Paul Grantham, Dave Freeman, Nick Fried and Tarik Sadat.

From the world of local journalism I have benefited from the assistance of Anthony Smith of the *Reading Chronicle* and Lucy Thorne of 'In Your Area' – the successor to the *Evening Post* - and very substantially from the work of their reporters ("quoted thus hereafter") and photographers whose work I have sometimes had to reproduce as best possible from old newsprint. John Bunyard has been as usual vital in the production process.

My wife, Christine, has shown forbearance for yet another football project, whilst willing me to write about something completely different for a change.

A final nod to a man I met fleetingly and once only, Brian Broad. A man of about my age, about whom I know nothing, other than he followed my team. For 30 years from 1964 he kept all his Reading FC football cuttings in good order. For the next 20 years he curated this pile of old newsprint, not bearing to chuck it away. It came my way and provoked my childhood memories of the club that I followed at a curious distance in the Sixties. I thought I should do something with this, I wanted to understand the puzzling nature of the club at that unsettling time. So here goes …

Contents

Introduction

The principal focus here is the period of Roy Bentley's management of Reading FC, the six seasons from 1963 to 1969. The club went through the familiar cycle of new broom, some changes, many promises, the investment of hope and money, excuses, failure and the termination of contract. Bentley's predecessor, Harry Johnston, spent seven years (1955-62) making the same journey. On both occasions the journey ended in the bottom half of the old Third Division. Reading had been a Third Division club since 1931. Ultimately the only thing remarkable about either of their endeavours was the sense of stasis, of nothing much ever happening or changing. They say in football, if you're not going forwards you're going backwards. But that didn't ring true of Reading, or several other clubs, in those days. They ticked along in a more or less stationary position.

The great bulk of any football club's literature is understandably concentrated on the glory days. A small amount concerns itself with disaster and failure. No-one, as far as I know, has ever taken up the rather perverse challenge of trying to find out why nothing much happened and yet for many clubs the world over that counts for a fair part of their existence.

The fast-changing mid-1960s period is just still culturally in reach for a number of readers. The amount that can be known about a professional football club at this time is surprisingly extensive. There was greater transparency about financial affairs and more authoritative and detailed reporting in the local press. There was also less to know because a football club was much smaller in scale, by which I mean financial turnover, number of employees and public presence compared with fifty years later. It is therefore the intention of this book to examine all the major working parts of the club in an effort to see why it was that, despite all efforts and promises, it resolutely stood still in a time of enormous social and economic change. It is also an ambition to present a microcosm of the workings of an ordinary Football League club of this era. So the first half of this book is structured around the key people involved, their powers, functions and resources before moving on to the season-by-season narrative.

Inevitably there has to be a personal element in taking on such an unpromising publishing challenge. I saw my first football matches at Elm Park as an eight year-old in the latter half of the 1963-64 season, Bentley's first full season. It is customary for the long-standing fan to say "from the first moment I was hooked". That wasn't the case for me. I think I regarded Elm Park merely as the local branch of, or outlet for, an entity in my mind perceived as "Football" which is what I really loved. It wasn't until I was fourteen, and a little way past Bentley's time at Reading, that I felt emotionally involved in their results. In the Sixties Reading Football Club didn't "reach out" to the fan; it stood there and expected attendance and allegiance. During this period I went to Elm Park only a few times a season, probably quite dependent on friends going too, whilst absorbing most of my football from magazines, comics, radio commentaries, Subbuteo and playing in the park, playground or back garden. Reading FC were on the cold edge on my football world and I caught a sense of frustration and complaint about them from passing adults, the rat-a-tat of promise-disappointment-promise-disappointment, from some of the moaners literally walking by our front door on their way back to town. The local press set the anguish in bold type. Followers, for some historic reason I could not yet perceive, were somehow thought to be due more from the town's team but the pitfalls that ended progress were made to feel inevitable. So it was each year; ticking along, stuck in Division Three once more, forever and ever. Amen.

READING
FOOTBALL
CLUB

OFFICIAL PROGRAMME 4d

Programme cover 1962-63

The Sixties – decade of opportunity?

A great many things began in 1963, certainly more than that which Philip Larkin, inaccurately, suggested. The Beatles sprang to national and then international fame. Harold Wilson became leader of the Labour Party and then Prime Minister. Each in their own field dominated the decade. Arguably the Sixties themselves didn't really kick off until 1963. That case could surely be made for Reading FC which found itself that year with a new chairman and a new manager, Roy Bentley. Bert Kersley, chairman of the Supporters' Club, "regarded the new season (1963-64) as a new era for Reading and the beginning of a five-year plan".

There were probably as many metaphorical as literal new dawns in the Britain of the Sixties, a decade characterised by social, cultural and economic turmoil, much of which the likes of elderly Bert Kersley would not have welcomed. From the distance of half a century we rather forget the tensions involved and the darker side of that decade. What few iconic images sum up the Sixties for you? It would be a surprise if any of your choices did not include the Beatles' Sergeant Pepper album cover, a James Bond film poster or Bobby Moore held aloft by team-mates in the late July afternoon sunshine of 1966. Perhaps an E-type Jaguar, Emma Peel or a shot from the Cassius Clay-Henry Cooper fight? Twiggy, Patrick McGoohan in The Prisoner, the Martini adverts – "any time, any place, anywhere, there's a wonderful world you can share, with the bright one, the right one...".

The old saying goes "if you can remember the Sixties you weren't really there" and in a way there's more than a grain of truth in that. The Sixties, in that cultural cliché way, really happened, it's said, for just a couple of thousand people in London. Half of those iconic images suggested above were purely fictional. No Martini lifestyle was ever lived in Caversham, let alone Tilehurst or Whitley. Sure, the Sixties had an impact, of sorts and partly resisted, on Reading, as we shall see, but it's doubtful that Reading had any impact at all on the Sixties as we've come to know them now.

Life went on in Reading, not as before 1963, but in a grittier, black-and-white, Cathy-Come-Home version of the Sixties. Slum clearances, casual street violence and drunkenness, widespread theft and road accidents, old cars abandoned in side-streets, the canal blocked up with discarded prams and, in the background, the flicker of monochrome TV skipping from the invasion of the Daleks to the Vietnam war, the Kray twins to the Moors Murderers, Alf Garnett to Enoch Powell and the Aberfan disaster to the Torrey Canyon sinking.

Britain in 1963 was in need of a change and who knew what direction it would take. English football in 1963 was in need of a change too and that was already underway, not that many folk at Elm Park, apparently still locked in a 1950s mindset, seemed to appreciate it. Recent reforms had created a fresh opportunity for lower league clubs like Reading.

Since joining the Football League in 1920 Reading's challenge generally had been to win the single promotion place available from Division Three (South) and become members of the nationally structured Division Two and thus full members of the Football League. The club's Southern League efforts prior to the First World War would have merited that status. Reading met the challenge only once, in 1926, and enjoyed five seasons at the higher level before suffering relegation. From 1931 to 1958 they were back, trapped in Division Three (South), finishing runners-up four times and coming close to promotion on several other occasions.

By the mid-1950s it was clear, even to the mind-numbed old men of the Football League, that divisions of 24 clubs with only one promotion place, and no relegation, were not a recipe for sustained season-long excitement. So, at the end of the 1957-58 season, the top halves of Division Three (North and

South) became the new Third Division (the bottom halves becoming Division Four) and Reading, who made the cut comfortably, now had two promotion places to aim for – as well as the rather distantly viewed threat of relegation. Of course, the same offer was on the table to other stalwarts of Division Three (South) some of whom – like Swindon, Watford, Bournemouth – had never yet played in Division Two and where the thirst to do so was at least as great as in Reading.

Another fundamental reform was the abolition of the maximum wage in 1961. From this point onward clubs were allowed to pay players what they thought they were worth and, whilst the main effect was felt in the higher divisions, it did allow clubs in the lower divisions with large gates and / or ambitious directors more opportunity to invest in the future success of their clubs. In 1963 a High Court case involving George Eastham gave players greater freedom to move between clubs thus further freeing up the flow of available talent, though at an increased cost to clubs.

Ultimately the effect of these two reforms was to favour the big city clubs but in this particular era there were, nevertheless, some notable successes for small town clubs like Reading. Burnley, a traditional club, won the League in 1960 and reached the Cup Final in 1962. Luton, a rather less respected club, also reached the Cup Final in 1959. More startling than either of these were, firstly, the rise of Ipswich Town from Division Three (South) in 1957 to League champions in 1962 and, secondly, of Northampton Town, the first to make it all the way from Division Four to Division One in 1965 (though they made journey back just as quickly). In terms of population Ipswich and Northampton had no more to offer than Reading and in terms of football pedigree rather less. All this, of course, was apparent to long-standing supporters, local journalists and, one presumes, the directors of the club.

So too was the continued frustration with "dreary" Third Division football, with meeting the same clubs year after year and with getting nowhere in the FA Cup. Yet when new club chairman Alf Smith took up his seat in June 1963 he spoke with the strained voice of past economies and concerns. "I fully realise the difficulties that lie ahead ... and look forward with confidence and I am quite sure there is a future in the world of football for our club." Just a year earlier Accrington Stanley had resigned from the Football League (thus creating a vacancy that Oxford United filled) on account of financial difficulties. Their overdraft situation was certainly not a million pounds away from Reading's own. At his first shareholders' meeting Smith maintained the message by stating there would be "no big fees for players" and it was the manager's task "to find the right boys at the right price we can afford". The mantra at Elm Park, according to one well-connected insider, was always "there's no money" even when the popular view was that the British people "had never had it so good".

Nevertheless, the ambition of promotion to Division Two was regularly courted in the local press and held by the long-suffering supporters who had endured a never-ending diet of stodgy Third Division fare. In August 1963 this was no ludicrous or impossible dream; Swindon and Northampton had managed it the season before. With the exception of Middlesbrough (1966-67) the division was not blessed with the company of fallen giants expecting a swift promotion back to the big time. In financial terms there was a reasonably level playing field. Talent, application and consistency were as much the deciding factors as money. Reading's home attendances put the club at the half way mark in the division. The club was neither rich nor poor in terms of the Third Division. They could have been a contender. They were a contender. But they, with Roy Bentley at the helm, didn't make it and this is the story of why and how and what it cost in the long term.

12

In Bentley's time twelve clubs did make it to Division Two. There were three main routes – play your way, spend your way or kick your way out. QPR (1967) and Swindon (1969) played their way out and were good enough to win the League Cup too on their way up. Bury (1968) and Hull City (1966) spent heavily and played some good stuff too. Coventry (1964) spent heavily and kicked hard. Crystal Palace (1964), Millwall (1966) and Watford (1969) all kicked hard. And there was one other way. Just happen to be in the top two when the season stopped. Promoted without any particular distinction and with slightly lower points totals were Carlisle and Bristol City (1965), Middlesbrough (1966) and Oxford United (1968). If their seasons had finished a little earlier or a little later it might just as well have been someone else's glory. There are seasons when three clubs might 'deserve' to go up and others when it might be one or none but regardless of that the Football League always had to promote two. And in case you're suspecting home town bias here there wasn't one season when Reading really 'deserved' to get promoted. In the Sixties opportunity knocked for Reading. No-one answered the door.

Fred May welcomes Roy Bentley to Elm Park

The new manager

If there was one miracle ingredient needed to realise the opportunity it was the choice of the right manager. It was common practice for the board of directors of a lower league club to appoint a well-known ex-international without any managerial experience to the role. To do so brought the club a certain amount of kudos and glamour, the potential of useful contacts nearer the top of the game and presumably a man who knew how football players worked at the highest or finest level. Reading had appointed the ex-Arsenal and England forward Ted Drake in 1947 and he gave the club six, mostly grand, years of service before departing to Chelsea where he won the League title in 1955. Roy Bentley was his captain there.

But this kind of appointment was by no means a fool-proof plan. Outcomes could vary dramatically. In late 1955 both Reading and Ipswich Town of Division Three (South) appointed members of the England defence that had been traumatised 6-3 by Hungary at Wembley two years earlier. Seven years later Reading were in much the same place as they had been when Harry Johnston took over. Ipswich made the better appointment in Alf Ramsey who won the titles of Division Three (South), Division Two and Division One champions for them in the same time span. The difference wasn't all down to the manager; the board of directors who appointed and nurtured the manager also had an influence.

Harry Johnston and Roy Bentley both had about a dozen England caps and each had taken part in a major international disaster; Johnston's was Hungary 1953 and Bentley was at Belo Horizonte in 1950 when England lost to the USA in the World Cup. Though their international careers overlapped they never featured in the same England match. And they were quite different as managers.

It was clear from the praise offered to Bentley in his early days at Reading in 1963 and the comparisons drawn with Johnston when Bentley left six years later, that Harry Johnston was a slacker, a man on easy street, happy to take the salary, enjoy the position and do his own thing. Besides his lack-lustre England career Johnston had been captain of Blackpool and a somewhat surprising choice as Footballer of the Year in 1951 when his side lost in the Cup Final. He lifted the Cup two years later in the famous 'Matthews' final when his team overcame an injury-weakened Bolton in the last few minutes of the game. Just six months after retiring as a player he became Reading manager. It was the only time in his career that the Manchester-born Johnston lived and worked in the south. He was charming, socially adept, well-liked and could talk a good game. But he rested on the laurels of his playing career, took no notice of developments in the sport or advice from those outside his immediate circle. When it was obvious that his time was up, and his contract was not to be renewed at the end of 1962, a suitably gentlemanly, amicable arrangement ensued. He then earned a few more bob attacking club directors generally in the national press. Former Reading director Ted Hillier responded, "sometimes Harry Johnston needed a stick of gunpowder behind him. It's action and results that count". The *Reading Chronicle's* generous verdict in 1969 was that "he put together a fine footballing side with no killer instinct". Incredibly he is still Reading's longest-serving League manager – which says something of the patience and tolerance of directors and supporters of that era.

Roy Bentley was the only candidate interviewed for the job as Reading manager (on Drake's recommendation?) and he took the role by promising to be one of the new breed of tracksuit (as opposed to lounge suit) managers. Earlier in the season he had been playing for QPR. His term of office began on 17 January 1963 though it was not until 23 February he could take charge of a first team match. Reading had nine

16

consecutive matches postponed in one of the harshest winters of the century. Bentley's immediate concern was a battle against relegation to Division Four, a previously unthinkable danger but now a real possibility. He instilled a more defensive approach and bought in a tough young left-back from Watford, Colin Meldrum, who turned out to be his best buy of all. The fixture pile-up left Reading with seven games to play in May, five of which were away. Three wins and a draw were just enough. Reading survived by one place and on goal average from Bradford Park Avenue who declined into Division Four, out of the League in 1970 and into non-league oblivion thereafter. Bentley's real challenge – getting Reading into Division Two – could now begin.

A Bristolian, Bentley had an extraordinarily rich life in terms of experiences. In part this was a consequence of being born in 1924 and living to the age of almost 94. As a teenager he would have taken that. Roy Bentley served in the Royal Navy on destroyers escorting convoys across the north Atlantic in World War II. The prospect of death at any moment from unseen submarine enemies was constant and would have given him a useful perspective on problems in later civilian life. At 22 he married Violet, they had two daughters, and he joined Newcastle United from Bristol City. He won promotion with the Toon and scored in the all-time biggest League win (13-0 versus Newport). A long illness prompted a move back south to Chelsea in 1948 where he was top scorer for eight consecutive seasons. His greatest moment at Stamford Bridge was the unexpected League title in 1955. As an international it was probably the goal at Hampden Park in 1950 that effectively knocked Scotland out of the World Cup whilst qualifying England. His playing career wound down with spells at Fulham and QPR where he experimented with playing in the half back line. At the age of 38 he began his football managerial career, which was to last almost exactly a decade, with Reading, in a determined, ambitious and hard-working fashion.

Bentley had a pugnacious, war-time, look about him, and more than a hint of a Bristol accent, but he had a thoughtful side to the way he studied and approached the game. In the 1965-66 season he wrote a weekly column in the *Reading Chronicle* which still reads well today and raised several issues that the game tackled many years later, such as professional referees, Sunday football, mid-season breaks, having foreigners in English football and the need for a minimum 48-hour breaks between matches as advocated by the Brazilians.

He took the Reading job without a contract, a year's trial period for both parties, but immediately concerned himself with the long-term future of the club, attempting a complete overhaul of the club's youth teams which he judged to be very poor and disorganised. He demanded and said he always had full control of team selection and tactics though the vexed issue of transfers was another matter. With his first retained list in May 1963 he sacked nine players, one of whom, Bill Lacey, became the trainer, and he transfer-listed Johnny Petts and Peter Shreeves. Bentley then rushed to Scotland to pick up two free transfers, Peter Kerr and David Grant, from the recently disbanded Third Lanark club. All this energy reflected well on him, and poorly on his predecessor, and a supporter wrote to praise him for "revitalising the club and lifting it out of a rut". AREFF, the *Reading Chronicle* cartoonist and self-appointed spokesman for the everyman Reading fan, proclaimed 'Let's back Bentley' and "blot out the disasters of the past". The honeymoon was soon over as Bentley came face to face with the long-standing realities of running Reading Football Club. There was, of course, a power greater than Bentley at the club; the Board of Directors who appointed him.

The Board of Directors

Reading FC became a limited liability company in 1897. As with all such companies the sovereign power lay, in theory, with the votes of shareholders at the Annual or Extra-ordinary General Meetings. Their votes, after 1948 it was one per share owned, determined the composition of the Board of Directors who then directed the course of the company's (or club's) life. These were the men in charge, to whom Roy Bentley reported.

In practice the directors were not much troubled by the views of the non-board shareholders or indeed the supporters in general. The directors, of course, were significant shareholders in a position to vote to defend themselves and their policies.

The original share issue in 1897 was far from fully subscribed. There were two, possibly more, short periods when a positive move was made to raise funds for the club by selling the unsubscribed portion of the issue; in 1930-31 to the general public and in around 1956, in larger tranches, to local businesses. Other than that, the popular feeling was that shares in the club were hard to acquire. They were not openly offered or traded. All private transactions had to be ratified by the Board. What new shares were issued went to existing or new Board members.

As long ago as 1902 John Rabson, a Labour councillor, had promoted a scheme, in conjunction with the then directors, whereby the ordinary working-class supporter could save, in order to buy shares in the club. By the 1960s this was clearly no longer in vogue. Investors of small amounts would create an administrative burden; investors of large amounts would threaten existing directors' control of the company. At various times the officers of the Supporters' Club had shown an interest in standing for the Board and it would seem that this was not welcomed. It was not until 2001 that the Supporters' Club, as a body, came to hold any shares. A significant portion of the share capital thus remained unsubscribed. Beyond the scope of this book, that portion was to play a crucial part in the failed Robert Maxwell take-over saga in 1983 when Frank Waller and Leslie Davies, who were directors in the 1960s, attempted to use it in support of his outrageous bid.

In 1960 Caxton published the four volume 'Association Football' which acts as a Domesday Book of English football at the time, examining each constituent part in detail. Of directors it had this to say. They cannot be paid for their employment; they are responsible for overdrafts and financial shortfalls; they should divide responsibilities amongst themselves for ground maintenance, property and insurance, publicity, hospitality and player recruitment. It suggested that men took on the role for the love of the game, enhanced local standing, the hospitality involved and a feeling of superior involvement. One third of the directors had to retire each year and seek re-election. The recommended size of a board, as each League club was "an organisation of some magnitude", was between seven and twelve members. Reading FC, for some reason, restricted themselves to just four or five men. In the period under scrutiny none ever faced a contested vote to be re-elected. Strange as it may seem, perhaps the tiny size of the home directors' boardroom, the inner sanctum beyond the visiting directors hospitality area, had something to do with it. "Hardly room to swing a cat", said one witness.

In 1963 the outgoing chairman was the recently deceased Jimmy Carter, proprietor of the West Reading Laundry. He had been a director since 1938 (at just 31), chairman since 1953 and, unusually for a Reading director, had taken a part in the wider football world. Carter had been on the FA Council and the Football League liaison committee for lower division affairs. He had also been a local Conservative councillor in Reading. Carter assisted numerous charities, notably St John Ambulance, and enjoyed his summer leisure as the Commodore of the Upper Thames Motor-boat Club. He was a picture of sleek and well-fed bonhomie who died suddenly at the age of 56 in May 1963. Old supporters will remember the giant navy-blue hoarding which stood behind the Town End from at least 1949 to 1972, advertising his West Reading Laundry. It is not known whether he paid a good rate for this prime space though at one point he did charge the club £200pa for providing laundry services, previously done gratis.

As was, and continued to be, the custom he was succeeded by his vice-chairman, Alf Smith, an erstwhile Labour councillor, Mayor 1954-56, and the governing interest in Smith's Luxury Coaches. Smith was 69 when he became chairman of Reading. He was a self-made man of humble origins who had served on the Western Front in the First World War as a mechanic and then set up in the coach business in 1922. The firm became a limited company in 1947 and transporting fans in the post-war period became a significant part of the business – 67 coaches went to a cup-tie at West Bromwich in 1948, for example. In the spring of that year he was appointed a director of the football club, then vice-chairman in 1954. By the early 1960s Smith's had a fleet of 110 vehicles and was one of the largest operators in the south of England. The company ran scheduled services to coastal destinations like Hayling Island, had contract hire to take workers to AWRE in Aldermaston and, of course, provided transport for Reading fans to away and home matches (the latter by shuttle buses from St Mary Butts and Northumberland Avenue in Whitley). Smith himself was a well-known figure in the town through both his business and the Rotary Club. He was always known as 'Guv'nor', a constant pipe-smoker, a keen gardener and, despite being tight with money, seen as a good egg, if a somewhat gruff old bloke. Each summer he entertained members of the Supporters' Club committee at his large house in Tilehurst and he took a keen interest in both ground improvements at Elm Park and "the match fitness of the players". His traditionalist outlook on life is perhaps best summed up by an *Evening Post* report in 1968 on his "curiously antiquated" office and his reluctance to allow that he was a millionaire. "Such money is largely tied up within the business", he said. He retired as club chairman in 1968, was made life president, and was succeeded by Frank Waller.

Waller was appointed director in 1954 and vice-chairman in 1963. He was a more conspicuously successful businessman than the other board members through his involvement with Adwest Engineering and property interests based on Woodley Airfield. Waller operated on a national scale and his company made pre-tax profits of around half a million pounds in 1963 and 1964. By 1980 the socialist press had him down as a yacht-owning, Rolls Royce-driving confidant of hard-line Tory business leader Michael Edwardes of British Leyland fame.

The other directors were businessman John Windebank (appointed 1954, retired 1965) of whom I know nothing, Leslie Davies, a former director of Tranmere Rovers, who succeeded him, and was the managing director of Sigmund Pulsometer Pumps, a major industrial concern on the Oxford Road; Duncan Vincent (appointed 1963) a keen and jolly hockey player who was a partner in the Nicholas estate agency business and Derek Baylis (appointed 1960) from the local grocery store group of that name who always wore a flower in his lapel. Baylis took the place of Ted Hillier whose short-lived directorship lasted 1957-60. Hillier was a bullish, impatient man, boss of a local engineering company who, it would seem, was quickly frustrated by the inertia and lack of ambition of the other board members and manager Harry Johnston (1955-62). He offered to lend the club £5,000 interest-free as half the cost of signing Cliff Holton for a late promotion push in 1959 but no-one backed him up with the other half. Holton went to Watford instead and scored the goals that earned them their first ever promotion.

The directors collectively met their responsibilities to the shareholders by providing an annual financial and chairman's report at the AGM. The number of shareholders attending these meetings gradually diminished over time from around 70 in the late 1950s to around 35 in the late 1960s as they died off, moved away or lost interest and were not replaced.

Often the most salient fact taken from the AGM, held in August, was the profit or loss made by the club in the past financial year up to the end of June. In isolation the figure can be misleading or meaningless; a profit can come from selling the best players while a loss might be incurred by long overdue ground improvements. But over a span of years it can be instructive. For the eight seasons in which Harry Johnston was wholly or partially the team manager the aggregate figure was a loss of £39,327, almost half of which was incurred through two disastrous transfers in his final season, 1962-63. Over the following six seasons the club made an aggregate profit of £19,546. The net effect across the 14 seasons of Johnston and Bentley is a loss of £1,413 per annum or £27 per week. Split between the five directors that would be just about a fiver a week and the club was pretty much in the same place in the League in 1969 as it was in 1955.

To read the chairman's reports, year after year, would tell you a very different story, even if they usually sounded like the same broken record. The finances of the club were always of "considerable concern", economies were forever being made and the lack of support at the gate often bewailed. Good players from other clubs could not be had at less than extortionate fees whilst the wages Reading paid were as good as any club in the division. Reading between the lines it is possible to discern shifts in the club strategy. For a while in the late 1940s and early 1950s under manager Ted Drake Reading were able to combine investing in the team with a good youth development programme. After Ted Drake left in 1953 the results tailed off and previously high attendances fell,

23

as they did all over the country. For the rest of the 1950s Reading became a selling club and youth development atrophied. Directors talked about a pie-in-the-sky break-even attendance figure of 16,000 which had never yet been achieved. In the early 1960s gate figures fell further and admission prices had to be increased.

The frequently stated objective was to return the club to Second Division football, the idea of the First Division being publicly inconceivable. It would seem that the directors' financial planning was based on hoping that a successful team would attract high gates, that the occasional sale of a good young player would pay for the necessary acquisition of a few older heads to guide the other youngsters, that a Cup run here or there would put the icing on the cash-till and that the Supporters' Club would work their socks off to cover any shortfalls. In 1961 Jimmy Carter actually said, "the days have long gone by when the directors could be expected to find the money out of their own pockets". In 1956 the share capital was increased from £6,000 (the sum since 1897) to £20,000 but there was very little sign of directors investing in the newly created shares. In short, the directors must have felt they already contributed enough in terms of their time, public profile and expertise and saw no need or obligation to open their wallets too in support of the club's ambitions. Their expertise included scouting for new players; their expertise in this regard was not of the finest.

The increase in the share capital in 1956 was justified by the value of the club's land, property and player registrations being well in excess of £20,000. These assets also supported an overdraft that in 1961 had risen to nearly £30,000. But the picture and the strategy changed in the six years of Bentley's management. Firstly, the heavy Entertainment Tax paid on football gate receipts was abolished in 1957. This made a positive material difference of several thousand pounds a year. But more important were the fund-raising activities of the

Supporters' Club. In the 1950s the Supporters' Club had contributed much in kind – in labour and materials for the rebuilt Tilehurst End terrace and finishing the roof over the South Bank. In the 1960s there was greater freedom for, essentially, low level gambling schemes, that is various bingo cards and jackpot draws which Supporters' Club agents sold in their neighbourhoods, clubs and workplaces and at the match itself. In the period 1965-69 these contributed an average of £25,000 per annum to the parent club funds (or £500 per week) and comprised around 30% of the club's non-transfer income. These agents worked no less hard than the directors, going door-to-door, pub-to-pub, week after week, to collect and consolidate small sums of money from supporters and townsfolk, in the hope of providing funds for the directors to invest in a better, stronger football team. What did the directors do with the money? They used a great deal of it to pay down a not particularly onerous overdraft, already well-covered by the assets of the club. One could argue that the supporters were paying twice over for their football – at the gate and in the jackpot – while the directors, self-proclaimed successful businessmen, were hardly paying at all. On the other hand some of these directors were salaried (doubtless well so) employees rather than business owners with significant sums at their disposal.

In the annual reports the directors created a fog of apprehension, a sense of imminent doom, a belief that the club had been losing £200 per week, forever, despite their tireless work. The wheel spun around without ever moving forward. The aspirations (not promises) were the same, the model was the same – four teams (including Reserves, 'A' team and Minors) through which young players would progress – were the same, the club's accountants were the same, the club's solicitors were the same, the chairman was always congratulated on the same excellent way in which he had handled the meeting, the lack of will, change and investment was the same.

Perhaps 1963-64 would bring something different? A new chairman, a new manager, a new mood and new prosperity in the England of the Sixties. There was a new Secretary/Manager too; it was the old Secretary, Fred May.

The tiny Elm Park boardroom

The Secretary/Manager

From the distance of half a century there are not many ways in which the ethos, the attitude of mind, of the club can be re-captured in any detail. The fixed grin of the chairman's account in the annual report offers one limited view. Another, more instructive, is the official programme issued for every first team home match. Both, doubtless, involved, to a considerable degree, the pen of Secretary/Manager Fred May.

Like many other people around Elm Park in 1963 May was something of a fixture in human form. Born in 1907, Fred May became Secretary in 1947 and was given the title Secretary/Manager on the day Roy Bentley was appointed team manager in January 1963. This was a mark of May's influence, importance and long-standing at the club. In effect, on a day-to-day basis, he ran the club as the General Manager. Before joining Reading he had been a proof-reader at the large Co-operative Wholesale print works in Elgar Road. His fanaticism for football was marked by becoming honorary secretary of Wokingham Town at the age of 15 and his involvement up to and during the Second World War as a local referee and an occasional linesman in Football League matches.

May has been described by some who knew him as a shy, taciturn, occasionally rude man, confident in his own knowledge and as straight as a die (not an especially widespread virtue in the world of football administration in the 1950s and 1960s). With his mild features, thinning hair and always dressed in jacket, white shirt, dark tie and pocket handkerchief, Fred May was every inch a background figure. From his proof-reading background he would know what a mistake was and from his refereeing experience he would have a clear or at least decisive view of right and wrong. He was an unflagging administrative workhorse but without a commercial thought in his head. He must once have given

Reading's young trialist inside forward Jimmy Hill his insurance cards from Reading and, now at 56, would look in amazement at the Sky Blue Revolution that the bearded wonder was leading at Third Division rivals Coventry City.

The match programme was one of Fred May's easier duties. Effort was spared, if one compares his output with that of other clubs at the time who would have no more money than Reading for any indulgence. To focus on the programme may seem a trifle harsh, a quest to make the most of whatever slight source material there is. On the contrary it can be argued that the match programme played a disproportionately important role as the public face of, or window into, the club. It was easily and cheaply available at four old pence (the price of a tabloid newspaper) and the club's only official and unmediated statement to the world. It had several potential audiences – the visiting club's officials, the football authorities, the home supporters (and sometimes the away fans), the Supporters' Club and its members, potential new supporters and the numerous collectors of programmes around the country. It had the opportunity to tell the world what Reading Football Club was, is and wanted to be and to shape its identity and personality.

But these programmes come across now as just an administrative burden to be fulfilled. The club did not really want to speak unless it had to. Care is taken over the titles and credentials of dignitaries; all directors are flatteringly 'Esquire' and the secretary of the opposing club (a Mister) always gets a name-check. Amateur players are given their initials in the line-ups. The repetition is shameless with pages of text repeated from issue to issue. Every visiting club is the well-known club from "___ shire" and every ground is "well-appointed". For 1963-64 a striking new cover design was introduced but the graphic device is a generic image of goalkeeper reaching for a high ball – and dressed as if to play a game in the 1920s! It was used again for 1964-65, the

28

change of season noted, and in neither year did the cover indicate the date or the opponents. That way some money could be saved by having exactly the same four cover pages for every match.

The first inner page gave the basic club credentials (directors, colours etc) and 'Elm Park Attractions' with equal prominence allotted to an upcoming Third Division match against, say, Hull City and a Hampshire League match versus Alton Town Reserves. The third page was 'From the Team Manager's Office' but judging by the similarity in style of Harry Johnston's and Roy Bentley's reports the words may often have been Fred May's. Here the focus was very much on immediate past away matches with all the bad bits from the newspaper reports cut out and the unlucky parts highlighted. "Our lads were not disgraced" rather set the tone and there was almost nothing about the general situation of the club, the division or the game at large. The pen pictures of the opponents were typically supplied by the opposing club themselves. There would be a league table, a fixture list with results for the first team and reserves, the half-time scoreboard key, a 'today's personality' half-page piece featuring a few facts and a head-shot, sometimes a decade old, of a home player. And then the Supporters' Club notes whose tone of voice has not worn at all well. It veered between the irate park-keeper ("turn up early for the cup-tie", "don't bring your car") and the obsequious Butlin's redcoat ("this is a must", "have you joined our supporters' club? If not, join now." "Bring your friends and cheer.") The rest is adverts, local adverts, usually placed by friends or directors of the club. Apart from the very occasional cup-tie the formula was the same week after week after season.

So, the programme was a good clue to the mental outlook of Reading FC as it had been for several years; very formal, clipped, entirely male in an 'officers and men' kind of way, without any sense of humour or excitement to engage the young fan or casual floating punter and often castigating those who crossed the pitch, threw missiles or didn't cheer. Was every programme in the country like that then? Thumbing through a dozen contemporaries it would seem that Aldershot's was worse, Swansea's as bad and everyone else's better. At other clubs there were more words, more photos, fans' letters, chat, less humbug, more wit, some design, some general editorial rather than a regurgitation of excuses for away defeats.

Programme ads placed by directors and friends

Whilst the programme may have been an unconsidered trifle May had other more weighty duties, principally keeping Reading FC afloat financially and on the straight and narrow. May was well-known and well-respected in Football League administration and gladly offered advice to his younger peers at other clubs. He had a deserved reputation for an extremely keen eye on players' and match officials' expenses. As Secretary he took the board minutes and kept the directors informed of the ongoing financial situation. His other key relationship was with Bert Kersley of the Supporters' Club. The Supporters' Club was of real importance both as a source of additional funds and as an out-sourced volunteer work-force of considerable size (providing for instance gate-men and tea-bar staff). Reading FC could not have functioned as it did without this support and out of politeness, if not necessity, Kersley sometimes attended, as an observer, the club's board meetings. Kersley had played a significant part in reviving the dormant Supporters' Club in 1954 and helped tide it over difficult moments in 1959, when two of its officials were jailed for fraud. He was a man with a public reputation, an alderman and a former Mayor (1947-49), and in 1963 became the (Labour) chair of the Borough Council finance committee.

It was always said Fred May worked tremendously hard and he almost certainly spent more hours in Elm Park than anyone else. In 1963 his own immediate, paid for, help was a secretary who was the wife of the honorary secretary of the Supporters' Club. An article elsewhere suggested that Second Division Portsmouth employed four men to cover May's various roles. His other responsibilities included drawing up players' contracts, providing match information to the League, travel arrangements for away games, communication with match officials, paying players' wages, making ticket sales and instigating ground repairs. Of the directors only Alf Smith, who sometimes paid for and supervised ground improvements, was often at Elm Park. The 'estate' of the football club beyond Elm Park itself was not very big. There was no training ground, no full-time youth development, no hospitality facilities other than the tiny board room, no club shop, just 300 car parking spaces behind the Town End and below the Tilehurst Road. The club owned some houses and / or maisonettes nearby for players' families' accommodation.

There was occasional transfer business to be conducted, signing on fees to be negotiated and living arrangements to be found for the incomers. More frequently scouts had to be given missions and paid expenses. Other clubs' scouts required complimentary tickets and there was rarely a problem fitting them in. There were typically in the region of 1,500-2,000 season-ticket holders who took up fewer than half the seats in the Norfolk Road stand. The season tickets were issued in cloth-bound booklets suggestive of some kind of superior membership status. The players' passes and those of the other friends of the club were similar in nature and closely guarded. Season tickets were priced in guineas, a posh way of adding 5% on to the price you paid in pounds. In town furniture from Wolfe & Hollander was priced in guineas, pilchards from MacFisheries not so much. There were no season tickets for the terraces; it was cash only at the turnstile and it was May's job to count all the money in on match days. For derby matches and cup-ties there was a good market for stand tickets for those who wished to watch the match in comparative comfort and dry.

These day-to-day administrative affairs kept May busy enough yet he also devoted some of his precious time to the Berks & Bucks FA (where he was on the governing Council) and the local leagues in the town. "I like to do everything I can on the amateur side of the game but, of course, one's time is limited. But if I can advise or help on a particular matter I always endeavour to do so", he said. He had his limits. In 1967 he had to ask the Berks & Bucks referees not to caution so many players as it was causing too much work for the disciplinary committee.

Having cut his teeth in football administration during the greatest attendance boom the game had ever known (1947-52) whipping up support for the club was not something that came naturally or comfortably to May. Small-size fixture posters – purely text / block capitals – were put up on a few street corners to advertise "forthcoming attractions" which usually included Reserves games.

If a badge were needed the town's coat of arms was borrowed, as it was for some of the new sky blue shirts worn in 1965-66 with the initials RFC superimposed. Fred May was the custodian of the club's history but not a very careful or curious one. He took ancient and faulty received wisdom and repeated it more or less verbatim in programmes and handbooks. When it came to the club's centenary year in 1971-72, with May still in post, almost no attempt was made to celebrate.

There was no local television or radio, let alone the internet, so the local press was of tremendous importance. The majority of households in the town would have taken one of the weeklies – the *Reading Chronicle* and the *Reading Standard* – and they covered the club fully and attractively with great action photos, cartoon strips and readers' letters. There was a mature relationship between the local press and the club. Each needed the other. The press had to call it the way their readers would have seen it and often used terms like "atrocious" and "lacking effort" but at the same time were willing to bang the drum loud if the club had good news or high hopes. Roy Bentley would spend an hour briefing local journalists and infrequently a director would give an interview but never Fred May. In effect the press was the club's PR department – but a relatively honest one. The impression was that Reading or its players were never put forward to feature in national magazines like *Football Monthly* or *Soccer Star* though May's connections with the League garnered some coverage in the *Football League Review* publication.

The club itself almost seemed to shun contact with the outside world on non-match days. In this, it was not particularly unusual. A *Football Monthly* editorial of November 1965 focussed on the continuing decline in attendances and wrote, with Hill's Coventry City as the prime example of reform, "until now just a blur on the terrace the fan is being invited into a cosy club bar for a drink or a meal in a warm togetherness … these progressive clubs have thrown open their doors to show the fan ground premises for years as impenetrable as Fort Knox … after 77 years of keeping the faithful at arm's length – having collected their admission money – League football is slowly, ever so slowly, getting the modern message". Unquestionably Reading would have been numbered among the Fort Knox clubs. In 1963 the main entrance to the club had all the allure of a back-street wholesale potato merchants and the north-west boundary wall of Elm Park was topped with broken glass set in cement to deter intruders.

The *Daily Express,* in the days when it was a great and well-resourced newspaper, sent its "Soccer Swoop" team to Reading in December 1965 to conduct a "special report". It visited the club's "compact headquarters", found that "the ground had the uneasy calm of a department store after Christmas closing" and concluded that "slim resources are a valid excuse for lack of progress over quarter of a century". A month earlier the *Reading Chronicle's* sports editor Roger Ware compared the airy offices at Third Division rivals Bristol Rovers' Eastville ground with the "cramped surroundings" and "two comparatively dingy rooms below the Elm Park stand". It was from here, with one secretary between them, that Fred May and Roy Bentley sought to steer Reading FC in an upward direction. The Soccer Swoop team thought that there was "ambition but not the right formula for success", that "three decades of little more than soccer mediocrity are all a string of well-meaning directors, officials and players can show" and that "the tone of the fans was not far short of apathy". The football club offered no comment in response.

Two years earlier, in October 1963, Swindon Town, freshly confident after promotion to Division Two, appeared in a charming BBC TV documentary *'Six days to Saturday'.* The cameras were given access to the boardroom (where a whole eleven directors discussed an Italian architect's plans for a cantilever stand), the dressing rooms, the players' homes (cue a young Mike Summerbee kicking a ball around in the street outside with the neighbouring kids) and even the aeroplane (!) bringing the squad back from an away game at Preston. The background settings were just as ordinary as Reading but the attitudes were a million miles away from the closed doors of Elm Park.

Fred May was a quiet, almost timid, man in the context of the football world and Reading had become a quiet club, a club without swagger of any kind. The secretary/manager beavered away in this quiet part of a quiet town, waiting patiently for success to come his way and invade his dimly-lit office under the Norfolk Road stand.

The main entrance

Elm Park c1967

Elm Park

Until 1943 the club had always had its headquarters or offices right in the town centre. But then enemy bombing destroyed the premises in Arcade Chambers, Market Place, and thereafter the officials of Reading FC resided, or retreated, to Elm Park a couple of miles to the west.

The Elm Park football ground was situated on the steep southern side of the Thames valley between the main westward Oxford and Tilehurst Roads and on the edge of a grid of red-brick late Victorian and Edwardian terraced housing. In the 1960s this would have been considered an ordinary, established, traditional, residential area with a mix of schools, churches, dusty sweet- or corner-shops, garage workshops, small print-works and a few green spaces. Built into a valley side and with its main frontage on Norfolk Road, effectively a workaday back street, Elm Park did nothing to impose itself on the passing motorist or pedestrian. Many townsfolk never knew it was there.

By 1963 essentially nothing remained of the structures erected when the ground opened in 1896. The oldest part was the Norfolk Road (or main or north) stand built in 1926 and scarcely changed since. It ran the length of the north touchline and had a capacity of about 4,000 almost all on bench seating. Cushions could be hired for a ha'penny a match for greater comfort. The stand was divided into sections A to E (running east to west) each with its separate turnstile, staircase and tea / Bovril counter. The pricing reflected the proximity to the halfway line with season tickets in C Stand costing seven guineas, B and D Stands six guineas and A and E Stands five guineas. The Directors Box, and behind that the boardroom, were at the back of C Stand. The overwhelming impressions I had as a small child were of woodenness and darkness, as if I was being led through a crowded, gloomy shed, smelling vaguely of tobacco and urine. The sudden emergence into the light and the bright greenness of the pitch below is a lasting memory. And because so much of my exposure to football by the age of eight had come through the radio the absence of a commentator left me quite disorientated. I had to judge what was going on for myself.

In the voids below the seating were the club's cramped offices where Fred May held sway and the dressing rooms and plunge baths, separated from the fans walking by in Norfolk Road only by frosted panes of glass. The players' tunnel led out to the pitch from below D Stand. Later in the 1960s various improvements and expansions were made to the stands and the areas beneath.

Looking from the stand to the left (or east) was the Town End, accessed from turnstiles on Norfolk Road. The northern half of the terracing was only twenty or so steps deep but the southern half rose to at least twice the height. The West Reading Laundry hoarding helped equalise the horizon line for a neater appearance. That end was favoured by those travelling from the town centre by bus down the Oxford Road. It was an open terrace dating from the 1930s, with a rudimentary trough toilet at the rear and a refreshment point in the far south-east corner. At the opposite end stood the larger, deeper but also open to the elements Tilehurst End, again accessed from Norfolk Road. This terrace had been built in 1957 by the Supporters' Club and was the most modern part of the ground. A tea hut stood right at the back. Along the south touchline loomed the only covered terrace, its roof finally completed in the mid-1950s. At the time it was known as the popular side or the Tilehurst Road terrace but from about 1970 it was called the South Bank. Behind the terrace was a large kiosk selling refreshments and old programmes. The total capacity of the ground was in the region of 27,000 but this had rarely been tested in the past decade.

The roof of the Norfolk Road stand had carried an advert for Huntley & Palmers biscuits since at least 1950 (and which lasted until re-roofing in the early 1970s). The South Bank roof bore an advert for Cooks Homes throughout the 1960s and other advertisements such as those for the Reading Chronicle, Baylis supermarkets, Simonds/Courage beers, Morlands brewery, Blakes Sports and Herbert & Lascelles were equally permanent fixtures in the ground. Herbert & Lascelles were the electrical contractors who installed the floodlighting system in 1954. Reading were relative pioneers in holding floodlit matches against all manner of opponents and were active participants in the Southern Professional Floodlit Cup (which was effectively replaced by the League Cup in 1960) – all of which helped boost gate revenues. The penalty of being a pioneer was that Reading's array of lights on the stand roofs and on poles behind the goals was soon surpassed by the new convention of a 'pylon-in-each-corner' arrangement at other clubs. By the early 1960s it was clear that the Elm Park lights were out-dated, dim and deficient and that replacing them would be another heavy bill to be paid. "The watery gloom of Reading's lights" was one reason why the club never featured in a single televised match throughout the 1960s. There was also no suitable and convenient point to place a TV gantry as pillars on both sides of the ground interrupted the view. Of course, this was hardly the club's biggest or most frequent problem but it was indicative of the way the club seemed set in the 1950s, at best.

Historically the Elm Park pitch, laid on clay, was often claggy and muddy in mid-winter. It had received the tender and expert attentions of Suttons Seeds in the past and presented itself well in the early season matches but it was subject to over-use especially at the end of season when it became dry, bumpy and lacking grass in the goal-mouths. Not only did the first team use it for training occasionally but it also hosted reserve and 'A' team home matches and a plethora of local league cup finals and benefit matches. In 1966-67, for instance, at least 75 matches were played on it. Surrounding the pitch was a dusty, red dressing that came off on your shoes but gave a stylish definition to the playing area. The pitch had a slight slope from west to east (the Town End) and the prevailing wind came from the west down the valley. Typically, therefore, Reading chose to kick with those advantages towards the Town End in the first half. Until 1970 it was possible for supporters to walk around the ground from one end to the other and a small number did swap ends at half-time to be behind whichever goal Reading were attacking.

As Third Division grounds of the 1960s went Elm Park was quite decent enough if unremarkable to the point of plainness. There was nothing in the ground indicative of the club's long history nor any club crest or club-specific graphic, nor any of the blue and white paint it later acquired. Almost all of this description would be familiar to someone who saw the last game played at Elm Park in 1998. The place hardly changed. Reporting on a match in 1996 *The Guardian* called Elm Park "a museum, fifty years past its sell-by date" which was a verdict a decade or two overly harsh.

So, if you wandered down Norfolk Road of a week-day afternoon in 1963, when the kids from Battle and Wilson Road schools were penned in their class-rooms (I was there) after the players had long gone home, and you walked by that factory-like main stand, you would get a sense of considerable quiet and emptiness. And if you hung around until half past five or maybe half past six you might catch sight of Fred May leaving, a bundle of files under his arm, as he walked up Parkside Road in the evening air back to his home and well-tended garden in Kenilworth Road on the nicer edge of Southcote. Meanwhile the hands on the clock over the South Bank ticked round and round.

Players and directors about to set off from Elm Park

The dressing room

In 1963 the club captain was the popular, wise-cracking Johnny Walker. Unsurprisingly he was the oldest player at an old 34 and the most experienced. He had played briefly in Division One with Wolves, followed by a five-year spell at Southampton and then signed for Reading aged 29 and had by now made over 250 appearances for the club. Walker was a proud and canny Scot who started as a winger and as he became slower made his way backwards to right full back. He was a calm, crafty and skillful player and his background was something of an exception in the dressing room. Before one away game his younger team-mates told the guy manning the players' entrance they were being bothered by an old fellow who pretended to be their captain and not let him in. On seeing Walker the gateman believed them utterly and it took some effort by the manager to get him admitted.

There was a dominant group of well-established, locally born, one-club men: Jimmy Wheeler, a 29 year-old winger, Maurice Evans, a 26 year-old wing-half, Dick Spiers, a 25 year-old centre-half, Dougie Webb, a 24 year-old inside forward and Gordon Neate, the 22 year-old understudy to Walker. All of these men were respected and liked by the club hierarchy and all went on to serve the club later in capacities other than as player; reserve manager, manager, scout, youth coach and groundsman respectively. To this group could be added forward Denis Allen, also 24, who had joined from Charlton two years earlier (and whose son Martin much later became the club's assistant manager) and also lived in Reading. These men and their families were great friends and had been around the club for years. Wheeler and Evans in particular were favourites of the fans. As a group they set a generally happy, relaxed and united tone in the dressing room and new arrivals and young players needed to relate to them. But their experience of life at other League clubs and in other divisions was virtually nil. The man who tended to their injuries – the trainer / physio Jimmy Wallbanks – was another familiar face. He had been with the club since 1953 and amused the crowd with his high-stepping sprints on to the pitch.

There were two more senior professionals of note, with the rest of the dressing room all at just 22 or younger. These two were Harry Johnston's final, some might say fatal, additions to the squad that he signed in November 1962. Johnny Petts came from Arsenal where he had scarcely made a mark as a ball-playing wing-half of slight stature. His was the kind of frame that was going out of fashion in a tougher football world but he was a big and lively personality. Roy Bentley never took to him and, to the great displeasure of many older-fashioned supporters, hardly ever picked him. Bentley found the opposite kind of problem with the other big signing who was so much not part of the team it's hard to believe. Harry Johnston had basically bequeathed him a Surrey off-break bowler / middle order batsman who might deign to play centre-forward out of the cricket season – and for a club record fee of £12,000 to boot! West Ham must have laughed all the way to the bank, having paid Chelsea rather less than that a year earlier for the services of Ron Tindall. Tindall had a Chelsea pedigree in a prolific goal-scoring partnership with Jimmy Greaves but at 27 was beginning to focus more on cricket. Citing a gentleman's agreement made with Johnston, Tindall turned down Bentley's request that he play in Reading's desperate relegation struggle in May 1963 and opted for cricket flannels instead. Nor would he return to a football jersey until well after the 1963-64 season had started.

Left back Colin Meldrum arrived in April 1963, a 21 year-old Glaswegian with an abrasive and energetic style that matched the manner in which Bentley wanted his team to play. In his first two years supporters voted him Player of the Season. With Meldrum, Spiers and Evans the defence looked fairly solid but somehow Bentley had a blind spot about the

43

goalkeeping position. He inherited 20 year-old Arthur Wilkie and 19 year-old Mike Dixon and could never make up his mind between them. Wilkie was thought to be the more agile and a better shot-stopper but prone to bursts of errors. Dixon was seen as steadier and courageous but had problems knowing when to stay or leave his line and was rarely commended for exceptional saves. Bentley played them roughly equally and then replaced them both in 1968 with Roy Brown from Tottenham who was not markedly better. Meanwhile the third team keeper Mike Walker left for Norwich and ended up with the best career of all of them. Amid all the transfer speculation that surrounded the Bentley years a goalkeeper's name was very rarely mentioned. Yet future England internationals Alex Stepney and Ray Clemence opposed Reading in this era as did other very good keepers such as Pat Jennings, Bill Glazier, Roger Jones and David Best. But Bentley's focus on improving the team was the forward line. The club lacked the big centre-forward around whom attacks could be built and the wingers to serve him with crosses. That was the way Bentley as a player had prospered. Instead Bentley's squad, as the 1963-64 kick-off drew near, contained four inside forwards / wing halves who struggled to find a regular place: Peter Shreeves, Ralph Norton, Mick Travers and Rod Thornhill, all aged between 20 and 22.

It was a disparate and somewhat tricky dressing room that Roy Bentley had to deal with in his first season as manager. Two senior professionals in Walker and Tindall with dramatically opposed commitments to the club, a hard core of local boys who would expect a place in the team by dint of previous service and who had the ear of directors and officials who always travelled together with the team, a costly wing half he didn't believe in and twelve lads who could still turn out for an Under-23 team. Not a single player had the valuable and instructive experience of ever winning promotion at other clubs to draw upon.

The 'squad system' had yet to be introduced. The club management and the fans thought in terms of the first team and the reserves and of players being assigned to a specific position and, therefore, shirt number. If you lost your place in the first team you also lost a sizeable portion of your wage packet, the bonuses for points gained and for the size of the home crowd. To be a first team regular was essentially to have a job as, for example, Reading's left-back and it would be the job you expected to hold unless injury or, rarely, suspension intervened. Someone else would have the job of being Reading's reserve left-back and would step in. Unless the form of the understudy was obviously better than that of the main man a change on grounds of performance would not be made. Dropping a man could destroy confidence as well as household income and would not be done lightly, especially to an established and married professional.

But reserve team football had a life and an importance of its own. Reading played in the Football Combination, an enduring competition for the clubs in the southern half of the Football League. Typically there were two divisions and Reading played in the lower. Before the days of regular, mass, away travel going to watch the Reserves, or the 'stiffs' as they were often called, was a way of the devoted fan getting a football fix on a Saturday afternoon when the first team were out of town. Season ticket holders could watch for free and others paid a reduced fee at the gate. The home club kept all the gate money and receipts from reserve games could add 8-10% to the season's total. Attendances tended to be in the range of 600-1,200 and the less competitive and sometimes more expressive play suited the tastes of the more traditional supporter who enjoyed a skilled and sporting contest. Reserve home matches were publicised on posters and in the programme and covered by match reports in the local press.

The 'A' team consisted of amateur youth players, apprentices and trialists and had played in the Hampshire

League for many years, there being no Berks & Bucks equivalent. This was boys against men stuff, the blooding youngsters in the world of adult football. Results were usually disappointing and it was a long and rocky road from the 'A' team to the first eleven. In this period the number who made it could be counted on one hand. In 1968 Reading left this competition to join the more suitable South East Counties League, an age-limited set-up only for Football League clubs. Feeding into the 'A' team were Reading Minors who played in the local parks league. The level of supervision and coaching was minimal and Bentley said "when I arrived to my surprise we had no coaching scheme or connection with local schools". In October 1963 an informal arrangement was struck to adopt Battle Athletic as an unofficial nursery club. One of their officials, Charlie Kearse, stated that "young prospects don't join Reading simply because the club did not project a particularly attractive image". There were piecemeal efforts throughout the period to involve players, and Bentley himself, in coaching groups of youngsters but the reputation of the club for developing young talent did not materially change. Reading's lack of a permanent training ground was an obvious impediment. The first team trained variously at Elm Park, Prospect Park, the Greyhound Stadium, Easthampstead, Cold Ash and at the directors' companies' sports grounds such as the Pulsometer or Adwest.

The demarcation between youth and senior football tended to be the signing of a professional contract but, as the Football League enacted a heavy registration fee, this step was not taken at all lightly by poorly resourced clubs like Reading. It was neither easy to find prospects nor to bring them through. In future times a group of emerging young talents was crucial to a successful promotion push (Senior, Wood, Gilkes in 1986; Hislop, Lovell, Taylor in 1994, for instance). Unfortunately, the Sixties produced no such equivalent fresh crop that could energise the dressing room.

So, the composition of the playing roster at Elm Park was slow and hard to change. Players might not be paid much but there was an implied security in their position. This was a homely club where local children frequently chatted to players in the street. They, and their families, were known and liked individuals, not mere cogs in a vast football machine, and decisions made on their status would have obvious and meaningful financial implications. Moving away would create domestic upheaval and probably bring a more challenging playing environment. Easy part-time work on the side elsewhere might be harder to find. Promotion to Division Two might offer the promise of more money or perhaps more likely the threat of not being up to the higher standard and consequently being moved on. Staying put would probably lead to a testimonial match and Dick Spiers, Maurice Evans and Denis Allen all enjoyed this benefit. The incentives to succeed were not as strong as they might have been and Bentley later came to the view it might be better to reduce the basic wage and increase the performance-related pay. In theory the simplest way of gingering things up was for him to buy.

The transfer market

When Roy Bentley arrived at Reading the club were paying no more than lip service to youth development. Peter Osgood from Wokingham (and later of Chelsea and England, the 'King of Stamford Bridge') famously called at Elm Park for a trial but no-one was in or at least didn't answer the door. Whilst Bentley had immediately set about a programme for spotting and training local youngsters he knew his immediate requirements had to be met from the transfer market.

As a club Reading were more dependent on the transfer market than most but somehow had failed to develop much craft within it. Historically directors were amongst those who scouted for new players (it was theoretically their money, so the thought was that they were entitled to an opinion). The secretary and the team manager were also part of the scouting team. By Bentley's time the directors were a little more hands-off but the purse strings were held quite tight – "the right boys at the right price" as Alf Smith had said in 1963. A year later the *Reading Chronicle* thought it was news worth reporting that "the directors were prepared to dip into their own pockets" to buy Maurice Cook from Fulham. In the event they waited another year and got him on free transfer which turned out to be the wiser move as he only ever made 13 appearances. The *Reading Chronicle* also noted that "Reading have never had a forward line strong enough to win promotion" and that was where the focus of the transfer activity lay.

Bentley hoped Ron Tindall would come good at centre-forward when he finally returned from the crease at The Oval and sought to offer him better supply from both wings. He spent his transfer budget of £7,500 on Alan Morris (from Swansea) and Freddie Jones (from Grimsby). The three men played together just twice! Morris and Jones managed just 42 league appearances between them before injury (Morris) and disillusion with the wages (Jones) ended their brief Reading careers, at a loss of £6,000.

Wingers were thought crucial to success as Don Rogers and Mike Summerbee were proving at Swindon, so the search for the right men went on long and hard. But Elm Park became a veritable wingers' graveyard in the 1960s. Meanwhile almost nothing was spent on defenders and goalkeepers. It would seem the directors were so scarred by the seventeen thousand irrecoverable pounds splurged by Johnston on Tindall and Petts in 1962 that they did not pay a five-figure fee again until 1968. In part this was driven by the fact that, for Reading, transfers were almost entirely a loss-making activity. In the period of Roy Bentley's management only two players (Pat Terry and John Collins) were sold on at a profit and only one home-grown man (Jimmy Mullen) commanded a fee. In six years Bentley spent approximately £65,000 on transfer fees and the club recouped well under half that amount. Bentley himself became overawed by spending what money he had, particularly when he had a budget of £30,000 in 1968-69, and was desperate to prove he could get value for money. Free transfers were another option but of the ten or so brought in only full-back Dave Bacuzzi from Manchester City was a notable success.

Adding value to players did not come easily to Reading. The experienced Terry and Collins were the only players sold profitably and then only to Third Division rivals. If a player was unhappy at the club – usually after wage negotiations or being dropped – he could put in a transfer request and it was an unusual week that no Reading player was on the list. Denis Allen and Arthur Wilkie made themselves available at least three times and the manager's star man Colin Meldrum did so twice. The club also transfer-listed players who were surplus to its requirements or beyond the disciplinary pale, with an appropriate fee attached for their registration. As far as can be seen none of this discomfort resulted in any fee being paid by another club for any listed Reading player. Reading found it even harder to sell than to buy and had to give away the players they no longer wanted or no longer wanted to play for them. Several went into part-time non-league football. Some emigrated. Ron Foster went to the States, Ernie Yard and David Grant to South Africa. Ron Tindall said he was going to South Africa, secured himself a free transfer on that basis, but stopped off at Portsmouth and made 159 appearances there!

John Collins signs for Reading as Fred May and Roy Bentley look on

Transfers apart, the other source of playing talent was the youth scheme or graduation from reserve football. Over Bentley's term of office thirteen made it into the first team but only five made more than a dozen first team appearances. Rod Thornhill turned professional in May 1963 and made 215 appearances. Peter Silvester, the star of this particular show, made 85 appearances in the forward line and was sold soon after Bentley left for a short-lived club record fee of £22,000 to Norwich. Ray Dean (57 appearances), Ron Bayliss (42) and Brian Faulkes (26) all later had short and unspectacular careers in Fourth Division defences. Winger Jimmy Mullen made just eight starts before being sold to Charlton, followed by a long career with Rotherham.

For some time the most Reading would pay for a player was around £5,000 and George Harris, Ernie Yard and Pat Terry were all successes at or below that mark. But rival clubs had the ability to pay way in excess of this. Hull City spent £100,000 on three players to help them to the title in 1966, Coventry, Oldham and Brentford were all noted by the *Reading Chronicle* as significant investors though money did not buy the latter two any success. The Hull City chairman, Harold Needler, was a genuine sugar daddy in that he sold shares in the family chocolate business to finance not just new players but new floodlights and a new gymnasium. The Tigers kept their Second Division place for over a decade.

Without this kind of largesse and with the flow of new blood into the team restricted, Roy Bentley knew he would need to improve those men he had in terms of ability, fitness, application and tactical organisation.

The tactics

The Sixties was the decade that saw football transformed from an entertainment that needed a few pennies to rub along into a business that needed a lot of pounds to survive. This transition caused major conflict between clubs, directors, players and supporters. The middle of the decade saw much soul-searching and bewailing (the 'soccer is sick syndrome') which was only partially alleviated by England's 1966 World Cup victory and the subsequent mini-boom. Going into that tournament the taste of English soccer was pretty sour.

The lessons of the 1950s imparted by the Hungarians, the Brazilians and Real Madrid were slowly absorbed by the English game – as well as being simultaneously and heartily contested in the floodlit Molineux mud where Wolves saw fit to crown themselves world champions, having vanquished various Continentals. Boxing Day 1963 was the swansong of the old score-lines. Results in Division One included a 3-3, a 4-4, a 1-5, two 6-1s, a 2-8 and a 10-1 (the last time a top division team reached double figures). Reading managed a modest 1-2 defeat but did win the return game against Colchester 5-3 two days later. The modern player typified this more casual approach to goals and results as belonging to "the Stanley Matthews generation". Matthews was the world-famous, Brylcreemed, crafty, dribbling winger, a winner of an FA Cup medal at the age of 38 in 1953, promoted back to the First Division at 48 and still playing at that level at 50. Thing is, Stoke only played him once at the age of 50 – against Gentleman Jim Langley of Fulham. He wasn't considered for Leeds, away.

As gates fell and wages rose in the early Sixties the need to find a competitive edge became more pressing. Though the tide was already turning it was Don Revie's Leeds United who famously set the tone. Promoted to the First Division in 1964 they played rough, methodically and defensively, upstarts upsetting the aristocrats from Everton and the like. Success almost followed. They might have missed the league title on goal average and then lost the FA Cup Final in extra-time in 1965 but they forced other clubs, and encouraged more, to adapt to their ways.

The new style left commentators, directors, supporters and some managers and players unimpressed. For all the changes happening abroad and the growing fluidity on the pitch English football minds were fixed on the old 2-3-5 or W-M formations. Reading continued to list the team line-ups in that way in the programme until 1967. On the pitch behind Brock Barracks a quarter of a mile away from Elm Park my first football lesson consisted of being told that players were either "dodgers" or "markers". The game was organised in such a way that each player had a defined opponent, as in our right-back marks their left-winger. It was as formal as a barn dance and if a team defied convention it was almost as unseemly as Black lining up with three rooks and one bishop. Stan Anderson, the Middlesbrough captain, drew out the differences in a *Football League Review* piece in 1968. "Ten years ago the game was slower with more individuality, but it wasn't better. Many players ploughed their own furrow, giving nothing to the team effort. Full-backs never went beyond the halfway line, wingers hugged the touchlines and centre-halves acted like policemen in the middle of the pitch. The work-rate now is such that the old player would be dead-beat by half-time and the old solo runs would be stifled at birth". Don Howe, then of Arsenal, added, "once, skilful players could delegate defensive responsibilities to defenders but now everyone has to contribute to the team pattern".

Roy Bentley was a creature of this earlier era with his best playing days rooted in the 1950s. So too was Revie but that didn't stop him moving on. But Bentley was perhaps more in love with the beauty of the game and less compelled to succeed than the Don and his acolytes. Bentley came into his first managerial role without much, if anything, in the way of formal coaching qualifications. He was a good character, he'd played on the biggest stages and he could, he hoped, work it out for himself. There was not much assistance to be had at Elm Park and reading all the newspaper cuttings one gets the sense of Roy being on a lone journey. He never hired his old mates to bolster his position and morale. He took the Reading dressing room as he found it and sought to mould it into better ways – if he could. His favourite phrase of praise was "sound constructive football". He recognised – who didn't – that the team needed to play with more energy and purpose than Johnston's lot but he wanted to play as good a game as his resources would allow. He wasn't interested in having a team of kickers though as time went by (the sick soccer syndrome) his idealism faded somewhat.

Even though he'd shown nine men the door and signed a fresh half dozen his first dressing room for the 1963-64 season wasn't really his own. Only Meldrum of his recruits made the grade, at left-back, and on the other flank the ageing skipper Johnny Walker kept chugging away. Walker, Wheeler, Webb, Wilkie, Evans, Spiers and Allen were still the mainstays of the team – happier playing the way they always had. At the start of the next season Bentley imposed a new 4-2-4 plan but it only lasted a few games as the forwards didn't buy into it. At the end of the 1964-65 season Bentley controversially sacked the easy-going Walker (it was called a free transfer but at 36 Walker was going nowhere) and claimed he would be going for a more direct style, cutting out excess passing in midfield. Walker's riposte in the local press was that "all the ball players have been sacked". The cultured Johnny Petts and a couple of Scottish lads had followed him out of the Norfolk Road door. Stating publicly that "the game is faster and more technical" Bentley asserted his authority at the start of the 1965-66 season. Club discipline would be tougher and players would no longer be allowed to have part-time jobs. Bentley was becoming more pragmatic as his five-year contract wore down. By the end of the season a fan commented in print, "this roughness was never a feature of Reading's play until Mr Bentley took over". After a poor start to the 1966-67 season Bentley effectively staged a coup against the old guard in the dressing room with Maurice Evans being the most notable casualty. He now finally had the kind of men and formation he wanted – a fast-moving 4-2-4 and the press commented "it's a long time since Reading had a recognisable system". He took that system into the next two seasons where it gradually became more abrasive and added an offside trap. But still Bentley said, "we're losing points to sides that rough us up". Late Sixties football – tough gig – and still a section of the fans was hollering for a return to 2-3-5. But frailties in the team meant retreats to 4-3-3 instead and occasionally 4-4-2.

This shift in the way in which football was played in the Sixties had a profound effect on another constituency – the match officials. In the slower and less competitive era of the 1950s refereeing could be more casual and hands-off. As the game became faster, harder and more cynical most referees failed to adapt. One or two were almost famous for trying to referee from within the centre circle and the failure to keep up with play was a common complaint. In general, they were far too lenient on foul and dangerous play but occasionally inclined to random and harsh judgements in an attempt to regain control. Players, wingers and goalkeepers in particular, could be kicked out of games. A substitute player was finally allowed in 1965-66 if another was injured and from the following season to come on for any reason. Referees and linesmen did not work as a team but just met up on the day of the match. Ignoring the signals of their linesmen was a frequent complaint about referees, certainly from the Reading press. Of course, the local press would focus on controversial decisions that went against, rather than for, Reading but there did seem to be rather a lot of them, particularly in away games at promotion-challenging clubs. In those days the match programme listed the home towns of the three officials – as if this implied some kind of neutrality (though Reading had a bad time at the hands of a ref from Swindon!). It may be a bias on my part to observe that a surprising preponderance of the 'controversial' officials came from outposts in East Anglia (Yarmouth, Caistor-on-sea, Ipswich) or South Wales (Treorchy, Port Talbot, Merthyr Tydfil) rather than more populous centres such as London or Birmingham. And I can imagine Fred May questioning the cost-effectiveness of the awkward travel arrangements by which they arrived at Elm Park. Just a wild thought ... As in any league in any era players remembered and resented the terrible decisions given against in past matches and doubtless brought those unhelpful feelings on to the pitch when reacquainted with those particular men in black. Both poor and inconsistent refereeing made management and tactics more difficult whilst diminishing spectator enjoyment and enflaming emotions.

Whilst the professional player had a hard time of it on the pitch his life during the week was not overly demanding. Training during the week became more specialised during the Sixties and moved away from the old 'ten laps around the pitch and a bit of shooting'. In his *Reading Chronicle* column in February 1966 Roy Bentley described a typical mid-season week. Monday - 10am-12pm, an easing out period designed to get rid of soreness, aches and pains. Tuesday – a hard session including a full-scale practice match, over by 12.30pm. Wednesday – a day's golf at Streatley, most play 36 holes. Thursday – a hard session of 40 minutes non-stop running to a set schedule of variation of pace, alterations of direction, quick twists and turns and finishing with timed sprints. Friday – first team players have the day off, a new part of the plan, to keep them rested and keen for Saturday.

It's easy to see why players, especially reserves, with time and energy on their hands and low wages in their pockets were interested in part-time jobs. During the summer many players worked as painters and decorators for local building firms whose bosses were friends of the club.

Team formations were practised in training but coaching as such, developing and improving skills and detailed consideration of next opponents' strengths and weaknesses were not really on the schedule. It was not until 1968 that Reading appointed someone to the title of coach (Ray Henderson). Hitherto Bentley's assistance came from the trainer and the assistant manager.

Overall there was a belief it was still all about getting the right players in the right positions and playing with determination. This last aspect was surprisingly problematic. There were numerous match reports in the *Reading Chronicle* of away games where the team or, more usually, the forwards were plainly accused of not trying. On several occasions Bentley himself joined in the public criticism. No explanation was offered for the lack of effort so one has to infer that either certain players were not very committed to the mission or were simply physically intimidated by the opposition – or both. A broken leg could cost you your career and, effectively, your house. Yet there were plenty of times when the reporters covering Reading's opponents said "you're the best team we've seen all season" and plenty of occasions, often in the Cups, when Reading rose to the occasion and put in a great performance. The promise of great things to come was always there so the disappointment was all the more bitter when they didn't arrive. That gap between promise and fulfilment created an awkward relationship between the club and the fans.

The big cup-ties

In describing the life and situation of Reading FC in the Sixties it would be quite remiss not to give a place of prominence to the big cup-ties. If Third Division football was the bread and butter, or stale bread and marge as some would have it, of an unambitious club then the big cup-ties were the jam, the cake and the icing. In theory it was possible for every club to have left Division Three through promotion or relegation in just four years. Complete change of menu. In practice Reading were one of eight clubs that stayed in the Division throughout Bentley's period in office. Bournemouth, Bristol Rovers, Watford, Shrewsbury, Walsall, Mansfield and Oldham visited Elm Park every year. Gillingham and Peterborough each missed just one season. It was a familiar diet.

In those days the FA Cup had a huge importance. The Final was the most previewed and garlanded match in the domestic calendar and the road to Wembley was paved with drama, upset, unexpected and heroic deeds, glory, cash, shame and sudden, ephemeral fame. By the time Reading joined the FA Cup trail, in the 1st Round usually held in mid-November, hopes of promotion were already indistinct. The club was never in the top two, the promotion places, after Guy Fawkes night. The FA Cup offered the opportunity to extend the excitement of the season for another two or three months. It added colour, hope and variety to the fixture list. Thousands waited with bated breath for the draw for the 3rd Round broadcast live on the radio in hushed tones from FA headquarters in Lancaster Gate on a Monday lunchtime. For players and fans alike it was a shot at the big time, the chance of a full Elm Park, national newspaper interest and the possibility of TV coverage or a giant-killing story to be re-told for decades to come.

For all this to work Reading had to reach the 3rd Round, the point when the First Division clubs entered the draw for the first time. Statistically, all teams in the first two rounds being equal, Reading's chance of drawing a First Division club at home in the 3rd Round were about 5% or, to put it another way, once in 20 years. And, in fact, those odds were spot-on. Between 1946 and 1965 the Biscuitmen's only such encounter had been against Manchester United in 1955, a tie lost after a replay.

There had been no cup glory under Harry Johnston. There had been no cup glory for a long time; not past the 3rd Round since 1935, not beaten a top division club since 1929 (Sheffield Wednesday). Roy Bentley's Reading managed to break a few of those ducks and put some cup cash in the club's coffers. The old saw about the chairman wanting a draw and the takings from a replay rather than a victory sometimes had a grain of truth. A good cup run or two could be financially transformative and it required 'just' the luck of the draw rather than the sustained performance across a promotion season. In Harry Johnston's last sally (1962-63) Reading went out of both cups in the 1st Round watched by a total of 22,000. Roy Bentley's best cup season (1967-68) attracted 155,000 over the course of eight games, creating funds that were spent on a new player who might have made a difference (he didn't but that's another story).

So, the FA Cup was important and something about the season would die when the club was knocked out. But there were always cup stories to be had and the local press played it big. There were double-page spreads with full opposition pen pictures for the early rounds, mushrooming occasionally to pull-out supplements with some colour photos and club histories. Injuries and suspensions acquired a rare importance, fears of the opposition danger man stalked every other pub conversation, while special cup kits were considered for their lucky omen value. In the Sixties clubs abided by the old FA Cup rule that in the event of a colour clash both sides would change, hence the unusual sights of Reading playing at Elm Park in all-white (versus Manchester City) or in red shirts (versus Sheffield Wednesday). The press always found an angle: avoiding the humiliation of defeat by an amateur club like Enfield or Dagenham; local honour and pride – tested three times against Aldershot and twice against Brentford; beating a jinx team like Newport County; or taking on the rarely encountered might of Newcastle or Arsenal. Whatever the story the local football interest would be piqued and the crowd numbers rose. For FA Cup ties at home to top sides ticket prices were sometimes increased, huge queues formed especially for the relatively short supply of stand (ie seated tickets), the Supporters' Club put out and sold trackside seats (chairs temporarily placed between the touchline and the usual perimeter wall, literally four foot from the action) and supporters were strenuously encouraged to get there early. Twice a special, enlarged, souvenir programme, at sixpence rather than fourpence, was produced to celebrate the occasion. There were hopes, more or less realised twice, of filling Elm Park to capacity for home ties and the travelling support for some away ties was numbered in the thousands.

The League Cup began quietly in 1960-61 with several of the biggest clubs choosing not to enter. Reading lost four of their first five ties in the competition so it didn't begin to grip the local imagination until a home tie against First Division Fulham in 1964-65. As more of the big clubs entered and a Wembley final replaced the low-key two-legged affair in 1967 the interest in the League Cup surged. It doubled Reading's chance to mix with the mighty and in this arena they had more success than in the FA Cup.

In total Roy Bentley's Reading played 42 cup matches, winning 19, drawing 11 and losing 12. Scaling that record up to a 46 game league season would give a return of 54 points which is at the top end of his actual league achievements.

Exactly a third of the matches were against Third Division opposition, 15 were against superior opponents (12 First Division) and 13 against Division Four or non-league sides. If Reading could have replicated their Cup form against Third Division opponents in the League they would have won the title by a distance! These statistics demonstrate that Roy Bentley was a good manager in the Cups and that the potential of the Reading team to achieve good results was rather higher than their actual league performances. Most supporters at the time would sadly have come to that conclusion anyway without the need for this analysis.

Memorabilia from the Sixties

The supporters

In 1963 the Board of Directors would have had in mind, based on recent experience, that a good Reading side would pull in crowds of 12,000. If promotion were in the offing that figure might go up to 16,000. However, during Roy Bentley's six-year reign average League gates hovered around the 8,000 mark. Those who didn't turn up stifled the club financially. Some of those who did turn up damaged the club emotionally. It was a period in which how many people watched football, and the ways in which they watched it, changed dramatically. It was Reading's woe to be on the wrong end of these changes and to be led by directors and officials whose attempts to keep up were flat-footed. The club's support went into absolute and relative decline in terms of numbers and deteriorated in terms of goodwill and passion.

In the seasons 1957-58 to 1961-62 Reading's crowds averaged around 12,000, a little higher than neighbours and Third Division rivals Swindon. Then in 1962-63 there were three new local developments which at first looked like temporary blips. But they became semi-permanent features. As Reading battled against relegation to Division Four average gates fell substantially to just over 8,000. Meanwhile Swindon battled successfully for promotion and their crowds leapt by 4,000 and then by another 5,000 the next season when in Division Two. And Oxford United were elected to Division Four, instantly doubling their crowds to 7,500. Historically Reading had drawn support from south Oxfordshire and north Berkshire but some of this undoubtedly now went to the Manor Ground, Oxford. By 1964-65 Oxford's crowds were larger than Reading's and Swindon's were double the size. In Bentley's final season the figures were Swindon – 18,055, Oxford – 11,636, Reading – 6,522. Taking my cue from the local press coverage it's fair to say nobody bothered about Fourth Division Aldershot unless drawn against them in the Cup. But the comparisons with Swindon and Oxford, all places of very similar size, were very much a live issue and their figures were frequently reported in the Reading press.

This was a relative decline, a fall in the local pecking order. But underlying this there was a long-term national decline in attendances, particularly in the lower divisions. As early as 1962 the Board was conscious of this and the subject was raised at the club AGM. Increased car ownership and televised sport on Saturday afternoons were seen, rightly, as contributory factors. But there were more and deeper reasons as people had more money in their pockets and more time to decide what to do with it. This was the beginning of the consumer age; the Sunday Times colour supplement was launched in 1962 full of enticing adverts for a better lifestyle. There was a boom in home ownership and therefore in DIY and gardening activity. The birth rate peaked in 1964 (Larkin may have had a point after all!). Husbands had more reasons to spend more time with their wives, especially at weekends. Going to the same old Third Division football while the world around was changing was less of an attraction and it had to compete with many other sporting activities.

The doings of Reading FC took up less than half the local sports pages. Obviously, it was the most important entity but it's surprising to see how much participative sport was also on offer. The Reading & District Sunday League began in 1964, alongside two other leagues already based in the town. It was reckoned 3,000 people could be involved in playing, managing and officiating in local league football at the weekends and there were some calls for local leagues to be suspended when Reading had a big cup-tie so that the gate could be boosted further. Tellingly, these calls were firmly resisted. For all Fred May's extra-curricular efforts there did not seem to be much affection between the professional and amateur wings of the game in the town.

There was increasing pressure from the other end of the football scale too. The launch of BBC's Match of the Day in 1964 brought top level televised football into the home on a regular basis for the first time and whetted the appetites of some for a higher standard than could be expected at Elm Park. Chelsea, in convenient west London, were doing well under Tommy Docherty and became something of a draw on Saturdays.

Getting another thousand people through the turnstiles really did make a financial difference and to that end the directors were early pioneers of Friday night football from 1961-62. It was tried again in 1962-63, 1965-66 and 1968-69. As is instantly apparent they found it difficult to make a firm decision one way or another. Their indecisiveness went further for in some later seasons the autumn and spring home matches were scheduled for Fridays but the bleak midwinter fixtures sat on Saturdays. Inevitably this had the effect of disrupting the regularity of supporters' attendance with the sizeable contingent of out-of-town fans complaining about being unable to get home from Friday night kick-offs – and therefore giving up on the club.

But there was more than football in the winter: many bar-billiards leagues, darts leagues, ladies' darts leagues, ten-pin bowling leagues and table tennis leagues along with all the usual rugby and hockey. The folk of Reading and district did not go short of competition or sporting entertainment during the week, much of it satisfyingly based in snug pubs.

It would be hard to argue that admission prices had a negative effect on attendances. Prices were low and standardised throughout the League for minimum terrace admission. Half-price concessions were made to under-15s (the minimum school-leaving age was 14) but not, until the mid-1960s, to pensioners, nor to school-children over 14. On one particular count Fred May announced that nearly one in six attending supporters was a youngster, though how carefully the turnstile man checked the age is a very open question. I have seen a friend go through the child's turnstile with a handkerchief over his beard. From the 19th century women had always been part of the football crowd; the proportion in the Sixties would be about 15% but, unlike the 19th century, they would be paying full price. Judging by the pictures of the crowd and the names and addresses of those who wrote to the newspapers Reading supporters were a real cross-section of society; from council employees living on council estates to retired military men living in rural villages.

In broad terms it would seem that while match-going at the lower League levels declined during the Sixties interest in football in general rose. Match of the Day, and ITV equivalents that followed, the launch of new football magazines, the meteoric career of George Best, the so-called fifth Beatle, the jackpot winners on the football pools, the World Cup in England all contributed to football seeping through to mainstream culture. Soccer, as it was so often termed at the start of the Sixties, was no longer in a box labelled 'men only' and just opened on a Saturday afternoon. It was popular, it had a freshness; the crowds were singing and swaying, the kits were modernised in line with new design ideas, some fans even watched away games on closed circuit TV links in local cinemas. There were plenty of people in Reading really interested in the football of now, me included, but that interest somehow couldn't be met by what was on offer at tired old Elm Park. The directors, Fred May, Roy Bentley, the Supporters' Club weren't blind. They tried to follow all the trends – late, half-hearted, on the cheap maybe – but the club and its support wasn't on a big enough scale to make it stick. Mutton trying to dress as lamb as the old insult had it.

What made it doubly, trebly, frustrating was Elm Park's big game jinx. Time and again the team would be in a position to do something, to affect the top of the table, to win a local derby and they would almost invariably fail. Those extra 10,000, the ones said to be drawn in by the idea of good football and a big atmosphere went home let down, disappointed, justified once more in their scepticism. There *was* a market of 15,000 fans for Reading if only the club could find the team, the narrative, the emotional bond to access it. Over 120 coaches and two special trains took 10,000 Reading fans to Arsenal in 1967. Over 4,000 travelled to Manchester City in 1968 and 6,000 to Aldershot in 1967. Around 20,000 or more would turn out for Cup-ties against First Division opposition. Derby matches tended to pull in 15-20,000. A year after Bentley left his post Reading seriously challenged for promotion in 1970 and for half the season crowds were up at an average of 12,000. That was about the number required to make Elm Park seem full enough for a charged atmosphere. Despite all the social and competitive pressures the demand for good, exciting football from a motivated team was there in Reading. The supply was another matter.

What people brought in their heads to football at Elm Park was perhaps different in the Sixties. To my mind there was more a sense of spectating and less a sense of belonging. It was more about what happened on the day and less about what happened across the season. There was less care for the club as an institution and little concern for the mental welfare of its players. Players, both home and visiting players, were so much more the focus, the managers less so and the directors, rich old men in the background, not at all. Some opposition players would show up year after year and thus be an important element of the day. Many people found Division Three tiresome and they wanted spectacle, domination, goals and victory. Some, especially the younger, just wearily accepted it as part of life's faded tapestry like sprouts for Christmas dinner or 'Two-way Family Favourites' on the radio forever. The Sixties was a time when the old and the inefficient was being swept away and the spectators at Elm Park could swiftly be bitter and vicious about anyone standing in the way of their desires.

Referees, opposing players and most worryingly home players were subject to the "notoriously quick temper of the Elm Park crowd" (those last few words are the *Reading Chronicle's*). Ironically within a week of the Daily Express suggesting that the Reading support was "usually undemonstrative" the crowd invaded the pitch at the end of a match against Walsall (January 1965), assaulted players, five hundred waited for an hour afterwards to coin the Walsall coach, with fifty police in attendance, as the referee was smuggled out of a side entrance and sent on his way back to his Swindon home. On other occasions bottles or even more dangerously a metal plate from the half-time scoreboard were thrown and the FA ordered warning notices to be posted around the ground and in the programme. There was the constant issue of supporters from the South Bank walking across the pitch at the end of the match to take a short cut home, to the groundsman's fury, whilst toilet rolls were more often used as missiles than on arses. There were just more kids around in those days, swarms of little, unsupervised baby-boomers, playing he in the complex passage-ways of the Tilehurst End, picking up empty glass bottles for the deposit money, flagrantly nicking stuff from refreshment kiosks, generally treating Elm Park like a giant playground. You'd see the same swarms screaming unbearably at Saturday morning pictures at the Odeon or tearing down the back streets on homemade go-karts.

There was also very occasional fighting or hooliganism as we came to know it the 1970s and 1980s. It was just as often scrapping in the seats as on the terraces, but Elm Park was not a place of fear. It was more like a badly run school where the staff, the pupils and the schools' inspectors (in the form of referees) were mildly cheating on each other. But the club were not blameless in the failure to create a sense of belonging. This was a club where promises to invest in new players were rarely met, where the selling of prized cup tickets could be scandalously disorganised or unfair, where the public announcer chastised the crowd and even on one occasion announced a first team away victory at a home reserve match when in fact the side had lost at Crewe.

The lack of a fan-club relationship was brought home quite forcibly by the tremendous vocal support a number of visiting sides – Coventry, Millwall and Swindon among them – enjoyed at Elm Park. Away supporters often congregated under the South Bank roof where their noise would be loudest and at big games the Reading choir "under the clock" could be out-shouted. The first step to rectify this was the competition to introduce a club song. Announced in January 1964 when promotion was still an outside possibility it was finally launched at a rain-sodden home defeat two months later. The 5,500 there, or some of them, gave "Reading – you're the tops" a couple of choruses and then it was completely forgotten. The *Reading Chronicle* helpfully headlined their match report "Reading – you're the flops" and AREFF put the boot further in with a cartoon strip entitled "Sad all over". A lesson there for Lady Sasima!

As the song didn't work a more permanent 'Cheer Club' or 'Cheer Group' stationed under the clock was tried from April 1966 on a more formal basis and integrated with the Supporters' Club new youth section, the Blue Streaks, from August 1966. Estimates of those involved ranged from 60 to 200 and whilst they sung hard they weren't able to change the atmosphere or the noise around Elm Park much. There was simply less singing or chanting in those days and therefore the individual shouts – be they funny, sarcastic, repetitive or insulting – made more of an impact. The bigger influence, in the wrong way, was the fans who picked on players they didn't like and badly affected their confidence. Alan Scarrott, for example, at times faced "the persistently cruel jibes of the crowd". It got to the point where Roy Bentley withdrew players from the team for their own good and was reluctant to blood youngsters in home matches.

It's quite difficult to understand the nature of the Reading crowd in the 1960s. Heck, thinking about it for the first time I struggle to make out my own attitude to the club back then. But the volatile relationship between club and crowd played a significant part in this narrative and said something about the kind of club and town that Reading was then and what Bentley had to deal with. Yet supporters I've spoken to very recently remember almost nothing of this.

Let's finish with a couple of quotes from Roy Bentley, made just months apart. After the League Cup defeat at Arsenal in October 1967 he said, "we're proud of them ... it was tremendously moving to hear that deafening chant every time we attacked". Six months later he told the *Chronicle* that the Reading support, "was the worst he has ever come across in his football career. Reading has never had a noisy or biased crowd but now it is getting ridiculous. There was hardly a whimper of support for us when we had shots bouncing off the cross-bar".

Hold those two thoughts as we spin forward to the autumn of 1968 and the correspondence columns of the *Reading Chronicle* after another big let-down at Elm Park against Swindon. One spectator questioned whether Reading should cater for the "5,000 fanatics" who are happy with "abysmal rubbish" or "chase the 10-15,000 real football supporters who will only pay to watch football of a reasonable standard?" Not surprisingly one of the fanatical 5,000 wrote back to following week to say, "if it were not for us there wouldn't be a club at all in this town. At least it gives you and your so-called 10,000 real supporters somewhere to go when the FA Cup or derby matches are played".

Maybe there is a truth in both of those letters. In effect Reading had two crowds, two types of support, both necessary but both in their different ways damaging in their presence and absence. The 5,123 (as it happens) fanatics present to witness the home defeat by Oldham that led to Bentley calling them the worst crowd he had ever known clearly weren't happy with their "abysmal rubbish". Meanwhile the first letter-writer was probably among the 10,000 Reading fans who travelled to the big cup-tie at Highbury but was happily absent when the likes of Oldham came visiting.

Stood between the stuffy and uncommunicative football club and the jaundiced and indifferent mass of support was the important institution of the Supporters' Club. Besides its crucial contributions of finance and labour the Supporters' Club was needed to offer energy, initiative and salve. In a difficult situation and a changing era how far could it live up to its motto "to help not hinder"?

The Supporters' Club

The Reading Football Supporters' Club (RFSC) played a large part in the life of the club, if not in the lives of that many of its fans. Its notes appeared in every programme, its members ran and served in the numerous programme shops and refreshment kiosks, it produced the club handbook and the enamel badges and, after the refurbishments of 1966, its name was etched in the glass above the main entrance and its initials were intertwined in the linoleum on which visitors first stepped. The Supporters' Club offices in the Norfolk Road stand were open five and a half days a week and from there all the various fund-raising schemes were organised. I recall as a child being both a little surprised and disappointed that the entity which produced the badges and the handbooks was one remove from the football club and not the actual club itself. Thus my, now rather treasured, dark blue oval badge said 'Reading Football Supporters' Club' not Reading FC.

Even then I sensed there was a lack of authenticity and when, about thirty years later, I became the chairman of that Supporters' Club I fully realised the difference between paid officials and players of the club and its volunteer supporters. It's similar to that between the priesthood and the lay helpers in a church. There is some kind of magic conferred on an actual player, however incidental he may be to the club's fortunes, which does not attach to a volunteer no matter how long-serving. Children see this right away, adults share this and directors and officials willingly recognise and use it too. So, for all the much work done and many roles played by the Supporters' Club it had very little direct influence on the major events of the football club. To underline the point about who had the power RFSC committee members were probably aware that in 1965 the Supporters' Club of Third Division rivals Watford was evicted by, and effectively marginalised by, that club's autocratic chairman Jim Bonsor.

Like any go-between, such as ambassadors or trade union negotiators, the RFSC leaders ran the risk of being more influenced by the party they were dealing with than by the members they were representing. Given the closeness of the financial and working relationships between the club and RFSC it's not surprising that many ordinary fans saw the Supporters' Club as part of the club hierarchy and therefore they were all too willing to express dissatisfaction and seek redress through the letters' columns of the local press. Because of their public profile and formal status the senior officials would almost be regarded in many quarters as one step down from the club directors.

In the 1964-65 handbook there are two small photographs which are impossible to reproduce. Both mimic the way in which team group photos were taken: in front of the main stand, front row sitting, back row standing behind. The first is of the Officers and Committee. All twenty, as you'd expect from that era, are white men, all in dark suit and tie. The second is of the Catering Staff. A gender studies academic coming across this, unlikely I know, would have frissons of both delight and horror. There are fourteen middle-aged and above women, mostly in floral patterned summer frocks. Strategically placed at both ends of the back row is a man in an open-necked shirt. And in the position where the captain would normally sit, centre of the front row, is a heavy-set man in suit and tie. Nothing could say more clearly – these women are under control. The more important and contemporary point which these photos make is that RFSC was an organisation of some scale, formality and access to club facilities.

Its chairman was Alderman Bert Kersley who was soon to be succeeded by his vice-chairman Les Lewendon, who ran a building company. In turn Lewendon was succeeded in 1969 by Jim Brooks who ran a plastering business. Membership of RFSC is believed to have peaked at 4,000 in 1957 and in Roy Bentley's time is unlikely to have been more than a thousand.

The cost of membership was a minimum of one shilling (at a time when terrace admission was three or four shillings) and thus relatively inexpensive. The benefits of membership were not clear from the programme notes. It may have allowed access to social events, various insurance schemes, a public draw for a couple of rare FA Cup Final tickets and the chance to become an agent for one of the lottery schemes; or it may simply have been asking for an act of charity.

The far, far more important revenue stream and the way in which most people came into contact with RFSC was through the various weekly lottery schemes. At one point 14,000 tickets were being sold for one weekly scheme. Thousands of non-attenders got to hear something of the club and agents made reasonable commission from the sale of tickets. Even some of the players (Dick Spiers, for example) were agents. From my child's point of view the whole thing was a mystery expressed in a code – the winning numbers merely printed alongside an amount (6377 £5 etc) in the newspaper or the programme. I never once saw a RFSC jackpot ticket even though, with my father's assistance, I was a regular contributor to the coffers of Littlewoods Pools.

Besides raising vital money by these means the other main purpose of the Supporters' Club was to make fans' match-going lives better. There was a social dimension. At the start of the Roy Bentley era every Monday night was Bingo night, with sessions held at the Huntley & Palmer's factory canteen on the King's Road and sometimes players dropped in to chat or take part. Every year up to 1967 RFSC held a New Year's Eve dance function at the same venue. There had always been restrictions on serving alcohol in Elm Park from its very first day but in August 1965 a Social Club, serving Courage beers, finally opened under the Norfolk Road stand. Initially membership of this was at the relatively high price of ten shillings, reduced to five shillings two years later and eventually incorporated into a raised RFSC subscription of two shillings and sixpence in 1969. One benefit of the Social Club was the occasional transmission of commentaries by telephone line from midweek away matches. By 1966 the Social Club was open Friday, Saturday and Sunday evenings on a regular basis. Encouraged by the possibilities and more substantial examples at other clubs in January 1967 RFSC announced plans to build, behind the Town End terrace, a £50,000 Social Club incorporating restaurant, large bar, dance floor and VIP boxes overlooking the pitch. "It's not a pipe-dream", said RFSC vice-chairman Jim Brooks. Sadly, it was, and the three-year fund-raising programme never really got off the ground.

Sensing a nebulous connection here let's leap from wine to women and song. It was thought that young female sellers of Bingo tickets on match days would boost takings. Two dozen "pretty girls" were recruited but this idea did not last long. RFSC by now were also in charge of the gramophone playing a mix of Top Twenty hits in the hour over the PA system before kick-off. In July 1967 RFSC staged a Freddie and the Dreamers concert on the Elm Park pitch but were dismayed by an attendance of only 800. The band had not had a Top Ten hit since 1964. Procol Harum's 'Whiter Shade of Pale' was Number One at the time with Pink Floyd, Cream, Scott McKenzie and Aretha Franklin (and the Beatles, of course, with 'All you need is love') also in the Top Twenty. Regrettably the Dreamers sound was not quite on trend. There was no 'vice' unconsidered that year; racehorses too! Foinavon, the Berkshire-trained, ultimate shock winner of the 1967 Grand National entered Elm Park on 14 April via the gate at the Tilehurst End and was slowly paraded around the pitch ahead of a home victory against Workington. The energetic and resourceful Jim Brooks instigated this publicity coup. I was damned impressed by such a touch of national glamour.

The football club took no interest in what we'd now call merchandise. It had no crest (the town badge being out of bounds for copyright reasons) and no design use for its given nickname – 'The Biscuitmen' – which dated from before the First World War. Other clubs took a much more proactive approach as evidenced by the adverts in *Football League Review*. The Oxford United shop offered 30 different items including team photos and car stickers. Mick Foster, one of the younger RFSC committee members, took on the challenge of producing and selling a limited range of souvenirs – pens, badges, pennants and the like – that would provide supporters with some kind of artefact to take away from the game and identify with at home. Many supporters simply knitted their own scarves, painted their own rattles or passed off Manchester City bobble-hats. The hunger for 'stuff' led to youngsters creating their own scrapbooks or collages from newspaper and magazine cuttings, autographs and match programmes. For the optimistic 1967-68 season, RFSC brought out an occasional magazine-like publication called Elm Park News. There were four issues and alas it didn't appear the following season. In terms of promoting goodwill there was an attempt via the Blue Streaks to mentor and encourage young supporters while ticket subsidies were paid by RFSC to allow old age pensioners to watch games from the comfort of 'A' Stand.

One fundamental aspect of most supporters' clubs was providing away travel but at Reading there was a particular issue – the club chairman Alf Smith owned the major coach company in the town, Smith's Luxury Coaches. It would appear that Smith's would run coaches only to some away games and at fairly commercial rates. Fans complained too few trips were set up and that they were poorly advertised – sometimes only over the loud-speaker system at the end of a home match. In defending the club and RFSC against the dearth of trips Bert Kersley claimed in 1964 that "there hasn't been a match suitable for a coach trip since Boxing Day and if the coach operator hasn't got a licence to run coaches to certain towns there can be no trips". Apparently, you had to seek a special licence from the Traffic Commissioner to go to places outside your region – which all sounds too East German to be true, but was in fact the case. The granting of such licences brought complaints from Smith's competitors.

In the Sixties the Supporters' Club provided the football club with a large store of money, labour, product, energy and ideas at no cost or obligation. It was far from unique in doing so and elsewhere other supporters' organisations would do just as much, if not more, for their own football clubs. RFSC helped to keep the club afloat financially in bad times and create a surplus in better times. It added, in its limited way, humanity. It smoothed the edges and filled in the gaps that would occur if all the club's affairs were left to Alf Smith, Frank Waller and Fred May alone. It was an effective, if unequal, partnership. The Supporters' Club could help maintain the club but never change it. It could try and cajole the mass of spectators but it was swimming against the tides of cynicism about the game and indifference to the club. Roy Bentley appreciated it and its efforts in his six-year struggle that started with the 1963-64 season.

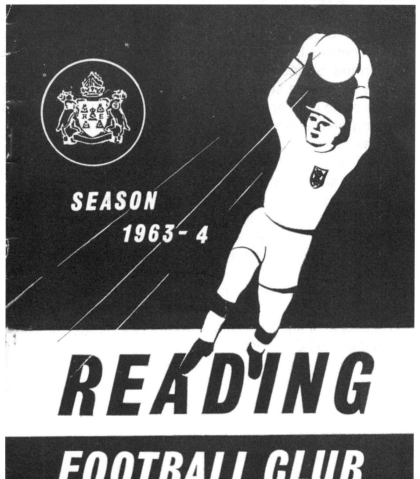

SEASON
1963 - 4

READING

FOOTBALL CLUB
OFFICIAL PROGRAMME 4d

1963-64

- August – first Ready Steady Go show on TV
- September - Harold Wilson's 'white heat of technology' speech
- November - Beatles dominate UK charts then take USA by storm
- February - M4 route debate – will it go north of Reading? New Civic Centre plans revealed; ultimately to be the Butts Centre and Hexagon
- March – pirate Radio Caroline starts broadcasting
- May – first Habitat store opens

If the Sixties revolution really did start in 1963 then Reading FC made a decent fist of joining in at the same time as the Beatles. Roy Bentley was quickly credited with "revitalising the club and lifting it out of a rut". Battle Athletic were taken on as an unofficial nursery club while first teamers were told they had to play for their place or lose it rather than expect the usual automatic selection. No other cultural force in the Sixties had quite the concentrated impact of the Beatles, in particular, and chart music, in general. References to hit songs crept into newspaper headlines, AREFF cartoons and even the Supporters' Club programmes notes.

Their secretary wrote, to encourage sales of Jackpot tickets, "so buy, man, buy your tickets, now 6d each". Carried away with enthusiasm the following month he shouted in print, "Can you write? If the answer is no then get one of our ball pens, they will write for you". And the RFSC range went beyond the new ballpoint pen. It's naughty, of course, to treat throwaway lines written in haste fifty years ago to such 'considered' analysis but even 25 year-olds back in 1963 would have been astonished by his next pitch. "Young men, do your necking in one of our ties, badges blazed and enamel all obtainable at our office". The aphrodisiac effect of a

79

Supporters' Club tie, I can vouch, is worse than nil. Be that as it may the Supporters' Club were working hard, handing over considerable sums to the football club and launching their own 10% discount scheme for members buying goods from local businesses.

Both chairman Alf Smith and manager Roy Bentley tempered their ambitions in public statements with Bentley promising only "every effort will be made" and that promotion in 1964-65 would be a more realistic target, though, as it turned out 1963-64 would be a closer call. Judging by the player ratings in the *Reading Chronicle* the strength of the side was in defence with Evans, Spiers, Wilkie and Meldrum the most highly rated players. Over the close season Bentley had acquired four new forwards in Peter Kerr, David Grant, Freddie Jones and Alan Morris thus creating more competition for the less highly-rated Webb, Allen and Shreeves. Bentley claimed he wanted "all-out attack" and a more energetic form of football. He transfer-listed wing-half Johnny Petts in July, suggesting he was not defensively enough minded. Petts would hang around like a ghost of football past for the next two seasons before getting a free transfer. It was a controversial exclusion. Petts' partner in the "1962 transfer madness" Ron Tindall went on to a monthly contract rather than sign terms offered and continued to play cricket for Surrey.

The idea that Roy Bentley was betraying a legacy of attractive, fair play persisted throughout the season and beyond. For all the praise for Bentley's energy there were as many concerns about the lack of ball players (personified by Petts and Johnny Walker). By early October Bentley was getting the slow hand-clap; just before Christmas the voice over the loud-speaker, after a home victory, told the departing crowd, "I should like to remind you that we are fourth from the top not from the bottom – more enthusiasm please". At the next home match the crowd responded by chanting "we want Petts" and the *Reading Chronicle* referred to the philosophy of

80

previous manager Harry Johnston as "an insistence on classical football, win or lose" – which clearly was the preference of a section of the support. Only when form picked up significantly in the New Year did the dissent quieten for a while.

Unfortunately, Roy Bentley's hopes were quite stymied by a difficult start to the season. The *Reading Chronicle* reported "the most misfortune-scarred pre-season since the war" with four key men (Wilkie, Grant, Jones and Tindall) missing and three of the four friendlies lost to lesser teams. David Grant was particularly unlucky, the teenager breaking a bone in his neck on holiday. Though he did have his moment to remember later, his Reading career never recovered from this blow. As a sign of his intentions Bentley dropped Johnny Walker from the team on the opening day and gave the captaincy to 'his' man, the recently signed Colin Meldrum, rather than any of the long-serving chaps such as Evans, Spiers or Wheeler. The more athletic and sturdier Gordon Neate replaced Walker at right back and Rod Thornhill made his debut in the opening match of the season at Millwall, for whom Alex Stepney was also a debutant. The tackling on the Reading wingers was particularly heavy and though the team fought hard the Lions won 2-0. The fixture compilers had not been kind to Bentley. In the first eight games Reading played away to Coventry and Crystal Palace (both to be promoted), as well as home to Palace and Mansfield, another strong outfit. In the first home game, against Palace, young full-back David High suffered a broken ankle in the tenth minute but played out the rest of the game (his last, as it turned out, for the club). The Biscuitmen dominated a 0-0 draw against Palace and then gave Luton "the luckiest point ever" through conceding a late equaliser at Elm Park.

There were almost 25,000 at Highfield Road to watch promotion favourites Coventry take on Reading who were clad "in a natty all-red strip". The *Reading Chronicle* commented on "the complete absence of the inferiority complex which has accompanied Reading to almost every away game in the past". Late on, with the game scoreless, referee Ken Dagnall controversially ruled out an effort by Peter Kerr and afterwards refused to say why he had done so. A great point nonetheless. Four days later an equally tough away fixture at Selhurst Park was lost 1-4. Palace were described as having a "rugged and at times over-boisterous rear-guard". Kerr and 'little' Freddie Jones were kicked unmercifully and Reading were still looking for their first win. It came with Tindall's return, at home to Mansfield, but that was the only victory in the first eight league matches and Reading were also by now out of the League Cup at the hands of Brentford. It was a flat start for the new era. Johnny Walker and Mick Travers came back into the team at the expense of Neate and Thornhill while fit again Arthur Wilkie replaced error-prone Mike Dixon in goal. Dougie Webb couldn't get in the side and asked for a transfer.

As September drew to close Reading were 20th, out of the relegation places on goal average alone, but Bentley had begun to find a useful blend of new and old and the next ten games brought seven wins and two draws. One headline exclaimed "free men win as £17,000 of talent looks on" referring to Petts and Tindall in the stands. Tindall was relegated to the reserves and admitted "I've lost my form" and was "unsettled" because he couldn't get a special contract that allowed him to play cricket during the football season. "Cricket comes first", he added while young Scotsman Jimmy Martin had his only good run in the first team in Tindall's number 9 shirt. Jimmy Wheeler was made captain for the day against Hull City on the occasion of his 400th appearance and suitably scored the first goal whilst the equally veteran Walker was back on penalty-kick duties for the second.

Port Vale decided to make a full day out of their midweek trip to Elm Park on 25 October. They stopped off at Wembley on the way to watch the 3pm kick-off between England and

The Rest of the World (Eusebio, Di Stefano, Yashin and all). Admittedly this had been billed as the match of the century (played to celebrate the centenary of the Football Association). Aged eight I was mightily impressed, not to say unduly influenced, by England's 2-1 victory. The Vale party stayed to the final whistle and found, due to traffic congestion around Wembley (shock horror) they'd left it rather too late to get Elm Park for the 7.15pm kick-off. While the Elm Park faithful cooled their heels the Spring Gardens Band played on – and on. Vale took the field shortly after 8pm thus incurring a massive £500 fine while Fred May had to deal with a number of spectators demanding refunds (result unknown). The visitors then played rough, had four men booked (a lot for those days) but at least had the grace to lose 1-0. The surge up the league table to ninth changed Bentley's mind: he was going for promotion this season! And he wanted a goal-scoring inside-forward to boost his chances. But as so often the finances were "very limited" and there came none. The only defeat in this spell was, deservedly 1-3, at heavy-spending, table-topping Oldham.

The 1st Round of the FA Cup in 1963-64 brought Enfield to Elm Park. Enfield were one of the leading amateur sides of the day. The amateur football world had its own leagues, its own FA Amateur Cup, with a final played at Wembley and an England amateur international XI some of whose players might also represent Great Britain in the Olympics. Because London had only half the number of Football League clubs its population merited, senior amateur football was strong all around its periphery; Bromley, Dulwich Hamlet, Sutton, Wimbledon, Kingstonian, Hendon, Barnet, Enfield, Walthamstow Avenue and Dagenham to name but some of the more prominent. In the Sixties Reading were to meet Hendon and Dagenham in the FA Cup as well as the "much-vaunted" Enfield who were thought to have a chance of knocking out the Biscuitmen. They played a decent standard of football and it was hard to entice their players into the professional ranks. Why swap a steady job and the generosities that came with amateur football for the boredom, fear, pressure, insecurity, dull training and excessive travel involved in being a lower division league player? Professionals resented the idea that amateurs could take the bread out of their families' mouths as well as the loss of public status that a cup defeat might bring. There was an edge to this kind of tie.

The attendance of 10,178 was the largest so far in the season with a thousand travelling from North London. The *Reading Chronicle* described it as "the most explosive match in years". After an hour Reading were 0-2 down and being outplayed. Then Mick Travers and Roy Thomas of Enfield were sent off for fighting. Any sending-off was extraordinary in those times; red cards and their frequent use were a thing of the future. Reading fought back hard. Enfield complained afterwards of "fierce tackling" as the home side levelled the scores. Then at the very end with the goal at his mercy an Enfield forward missed an absolute sitter and the tie went to a replay. This time Reading were the team two goals ahead but then pegged back. Extra-time and Maurice Evans had to take over in goal from the injured Wilkie. His brave display earned him the temporary nickname of Yashin. Under lights even gloomier than Elm Park's the professionals finally prevailed by four goals to two. The reward was a tie at "foggy, dismal Kenilworth Road" where a noisy Reading contingent (14 coaches plus) saw the away side one up with 15 minutes to play. A farcical penalty decision turned the game and Luton went through 2-1. Meanwhile Travers was suspended for three weeks. This harsh sentence entailed losing three weeks' first team wages of about £75 in total while the Enfield man lost very little in comparison.

Roy Bentley commented on what was dubbed "soccer's crime wave", claiming that "the game today is 100 times cleaner than it was even 10 years ago" which, given what else

84

he had to say during the season, was an extraordinary statement. Part of the issue were differences in interpretation and respect. Writing in response in the *Reading Chronicle* Dick Sawdon-Smith, on behalf of the men in black, said, "refereeing does not carry the respect it once did ... this is part of the general malady of the country. Authority and its representatives are decried and ridiculed on every hand". Even AREFF in the *Reading Chronicle* was getting down with the kids, calling Reading 'The Beat-Alls' and telling how they were 'Fab' and 'in the groove'.

Yet the supporters were far from satisfied. With Reading up to fourth in the table only 5,487 went to see the Biscuitmen win at home for the seventh time in a row on 14 December against Millwall. More letters came in criticising 'kick and rush' football, demanding the return of Petts and stating that "supporters have been brought up on classic forward play". The promotion form Bentley's Reading were offering was not enough for everyone. Two narrow away defeats brought Reading's run to an end but they still stood sixth when leaders Coventry City came to town on 11 January.

The Sky Blues were scoring at the rate of two and half goals a game and were eight points clear of Watford in second place. They looked uncatchable. Not so Watford for Reading were just three points behind the Hornets with a game in hand. There was a cup-tie level of expectation built around the game and hopes of a gate of 19,000 with 4,000 coming from the Midlands. In the event 7,000 Coventry fans gave their men "tremendous vocal support" in a crowd of just under 17,000 and they played superbly to take a two goal lead. But Reading weren't finished and fought back with two late goals to take a point in a hugely dramatic game. The Coventry support, and especially their version of the Eton Boating Song, inspired the *Reading Chronicle* to really bang the drum for Roy Bentley. A competition was launched in conjunction with the club to find a unique song for Reading fans to replace the standard and

85

laborious "2-4-6-8, who do we appreciate? Reading!" A 'Going Up' campaign was started with blue and white posters circulated around the town. The *Reading Chronicle* forcibly told fans to get behind the team. "Saturday telly addicts – if you don't come the directors won't put any more money in". As ever what's the chicken and what's the egg is debatable. The Going Up campaign talked of having a 'top beat group' play for half an hour before kick-off and all the first XI players of all the school teams in Reading were to be given free passes to the matches and supervised training at Elm Park.

Reading then lost at Mansfield to a penalty described as "peculiar". The next home match against Watford was vital. Reading were down to ten men after 12 minutes and up against Pat Jennings in the Watford goal. By a supreme effort – the *Reading Chronicle* gave every man 10 out of 10 – Reading triumphed 2-0 and AREFF called it the best days since Edelston (i.e. for about a decade). Now four points behind second place with a game in hand but the gate was still a shade under 10,000. Next up were Brentford who had already beaten Reading twice during the season. Keeper Wilkie was injured early so Maurice Evans wore the green shirt again. The referee was injured so a linesman took over and, as no-one else was appointed, Mick Travers, a non-playing reserve took over running the line for a while until proper order was restored. Reading won a dramatic game 4-3 and the *Reading Chronicle* said, "the courage of this Reading side is unlimited". I discovered over fifty years later that attending this match, his first ever, was the eight year-old boy who shared our twin desks at school. Clearly, in retrospect, not to be out-done I must have demanded that my father take me to the next home game. Little did we know what would be unleashed. So I went to the game against Bristol City and I remember Reading scored early and City scored late in a 1-1 draw. I was astonished to find in my research that Dougie Webb scored after just seven seconds - all downhill from there the glib would say – and indeed it was the case that Reading's form had begun to fade. A sequence of four 1-2 away defeats and a gain of one away point out of a possible twelve let the leading pack get away. Every defeat by a single goal – often according to the Press at the hands of the referee. Where was the away support? No coaches were running to these games. The reports didn't sell it very hard; the 1-1 draw at Hull was described as "lifeless soccer calculated to set the sparsely populated terraces yawning with boredom".

And where was the song, the new vital 'with-it' ingredient? They took their time drumming up then sorting through 200 entries before Fred May revealed, "I think we had to be up-to-date in our choice of song" and declared the winner to be a pastiche of a recent Freddie and the Dreamers hit 'you were made for me'. Over two months after the visit of Coventry City 'Reading, you're the tops' was launched as the new club song. It sank without trace, like Reading's promotion hopes, on a dismal, wet afternoon with a defeat to Oldham. Talk about not catching the moment.

The season petered out. Easter brought only two points from three easy games then Petts finally got in the team and Walker dropped out. There was a brief vision of what might have been with promotion-seeking Bournemouth vanquished 2-0 at Elm Park and promotion-seeking Watford taken all the way at Vicarage Road. Only a George Harris (!) header and referee Ken Dagnall denying Reading a penalty despite handball on the line saw them through. Bentley's first full season finished with the flourish of a 5-2 win at Bristol Rovers and a 4-0 thrashing of Southend.

These two wins pushed Reading to the top of the mid-table pile and a finish of sixth position with 52 points, eight points shy of Coventry and Crystal Palace in the promotion places (and also eight points ahead of 16th place).

The *Reading Chronicle* praised Bentley who "sorted out the wheat from the chaff and took them to within an ace of promotion". That was too flattering a verdict; eight points is not an ace away. The home form was fine, the equal of champions Coventry, but the away form was simply not good enough with 12 defeats in all. All hope had expired with 10 matches still to play. Reading took 11 points from the 10 games against the five clubs who finished above them; the ability was there but the consistency was not. The defence was settled: Wilkie, Walker, Meldrum, Evans and Spiers but only Allen and Wheeler appeared regularly in the forward line and the top scorer was the "mercurial and exasperating" Webb with a mere 14 goals. Bentley had not sorted out his forward line and it was their lack of effort and penetration in away games that had been most costly.

With a larger and more experienced squad the Reserves had a good year, just missing promotion from the Football Combination Division Two and enjoying several four-figure crowds. Colin Meldrum won the inaugural Player of the Season award. Walker (as assistant manager to be) and Wheeler (on the coaching staff) were retained despite their age. So too, but open to offers, were Petts and Tindall.

The Supporters' Club donations for the season totaled £9,000 plus £2,000 in kind for ground improvements while the Bingo schemes carried on through the summer with the attractive prize of a fashionable Mini car. At the AGM in September the football club announced a profit of £2,900.

On the whole it had been a promising first shot by the novice manager. His view was "after running for promotion for quite a time the team finished sixth. It was nothing sensational but it showed Division Two football was a very definite for the near future". He considered his 'trial period' to be at an end and asked the Board for a five-year contract, hoping at least to settle on three years. Their best offer was two years so Bentley went into the 1964-65 season without a contract but with some credit to his reputation.

Reading versus Oldham in the rain

89

SEASON
1964-5

REA*D*ING

FOOTBALL CLUB
OFFICIAL PROGRAMME 4d

1964-65

- August – BBC Match of the Day launched
- October – Labour narrowly win General Election
- December – abolition of death penalty
- December – a record 100 million-plus records sold in 1964
- January – Sir Winston Churchill's state funeral
- April – Mary Whitehouse sets up anti-permissive media group

Britain was modernising. Parlours were being knocked into through-lounges, terraced slums were being replaced by concrete tower blocks, skirts were shorter, hair was longer and the tweedy aristocratic Conservative Alec Douglas-Home was soon to be ousted as Prime Minister by the technocratic-minded Socialist Harold Wilson. Reading FC too were trying to progress. Alf Smith, chairman, stated "Reading have been in the Third Division far too long" while the *Reading Standard* saw a financial imperative in the need to move up. "For the last 33 years Reading have jogged along in the Third Division. Failure to win promotion has created larger and larger gaps on the terraces and now the club opens its League programme with the very real threat of extinction over its head".

The threat of extinction was surely exaggerated but the relative success of the previous season had resulted in an increase of only 250 on the average gate and the need to replace the ageing floodlight system was a considerable concern. Two clubs had already been refused permission by the League to use sub-standard lights. Wilkie, Kerr and Grant were in wage dispute with the club and Jones had already left for better pay elsewhere. One extremely quiet director, John Windebank, resigned to be replaced by another, Leslie Davies – probably a friend of Frank Waller's from the engineering industry – but another man on a salary rather than of independent means. Admission prices to the terraces were raised from three shillings to four shillings but there was no increase for the patrons in the stands even though this was thought by many young fans to be the domain of the 'rich people'.

The *Reading Standard* commented that "Reading have never had a forward line strong enough to win promotion". To remedy that failing Roy Bentley signed outside-right Mike Fairchild from Luton on a free transfer and centre-forward Pat Terry from Millwall for £2,000. The latter was one of Bentley's best pieces of business. Terry was a shock-haired, fiery leader of the attack, very good in the air and a dominating personality on the pitch – perhaps the Reading player in his time closest to Bentley's own style of play. Ron Tindall was gone but the rest of the seniors in the dressing room looked much the same: Walker, Wheeler, Wilkie, Webb, Evans, Allen, Spiers, Travers, Meldrum.

Terry for Tindall was a big improvement, Fairchild for Jones was neither here nor there. Bentley hoped that a switch to a 4-2-4 formation and more direct play would make the crucial difference. Both the local press and the match programme continued to list the line-ups in 2-3-5 formation and it didn't seem the forward players believed in the new system either. In the fourth game Reading were slaughtered 0-4 at Shrewsbury and the forwards were accused of not easing the pressure on the defence. Neate, "a much fitter alternative", came in for Walker who was really showing his age and the enthusiastic Wheeler replaced Fairchild at Barnsley. Wheeler broke his leg and his season was virtually over. Terry was then sent off at QPR but Reading did win. Then in the next away game Neate was badly injured at Walsall and his career was virtually over. For all that misfortune Reading were still bang on the heels on the leaders. By mid-October Reading were fourth in the table, a point off the top and Bentley was being courted by Watford for their managerial post.

Yet two old flaws still came to the fore. Effort and resource. At Bristol City (0-2) it was "the usual dreary away form" where "the forwards hardly raised a sweat". Bentley needed "to coax the players into showing the same urgency and determination away from home". Already without Wheeler and Neate, Pat Terry missed two games through suspension (both lost) and injured Maurice Evans missed 15 League games only one of which was won. "Without Terry and Evans Reading are a team without heart" claimed the press and even Bentley decried the lack of effort from his players in the club programme.

It was a busy October with 11 matches in all, featuring 3 wins, 3 defeats and 5 draws. Yet amid all the struggle and set-backs there was glory. With Reading's financial problems to the fore the importance of the cup competitions grew. Fortunately, in terms of making money if not conserving energy, Reading were to play 10 cup matches in all across the season. A bye and a 4-0 home win over QPR brought Reading to the 3rd Round of the League Cup and a home tie against "star-spangled" Fulham of the First Division. The Londoners fielded five internationals (but disappointingly not Johnny Haynes) and Rodney Marsh and 13,873 came to watch, including me for my first floodlit treat and first time on the South Bank. Fulham scored an easy goal after four minutes and a sigh of deflation went around Elm Park. Reading had a patched-up team – Petts in for Evans, Grant for Terry, Bridger for Walker – but hung on and eventually fought back. In the 71st minute Travers beat George Cohen on the left and centred for Meldrum to score with a stunning near post header amid frenzied scenes. No-one gave Reading much chance in the replay. Only 5,000 turned up at Craven Cottage, including a few hundred from Berkshire. Pat Terry was back in the team and together upfront with David Grant they worked the miracle. Grant scored early with a diving header, Travers added a

93

second just after the break and then Grant tapped in the third a minute later. Though Bobby Robson pulled one back the tie went to the visitors and hundreds poured across the pitch to congratulate the winners. It was Reading's first win over top-flight opposition for 34 years and the reward was a tie against Aston Villa. Only 8,000 showed up at Villa Park for "an apology of a cup-tie" and Reading, with "no Third Division bash" and "impeccable manners" went down 1-3 in the 4th Round.

Whether it was the distraction of the Cups or injuries Reading went on a nine-game winless spell in the League. Peter Knight was signed from Oxford United to play on the right wing but had no positive impact as the Biscuitmen lost touch with the leaders. Pat Terry's ankle had been fractured by Gater of Bournemouth – "where the centre-half kicked there was no ball" said Bentley, diplomatically. By mid-December the gap was eight points to Bristol Rovers and Grimsby and Bentley's men were halfway down the table. But they were in the 2nd Round of the FA Cup, drawn away to local rivals Aldershot. To be fair this was a rivalry more keenly felt in North Hampshire than in Berkshire where the Shots those days were regarded as small fry. "Aldershot are not a good side and we can beat them", said Bentley confidently and in front of 3,000 travelling fans he was proved right. The draw for the 3rd Round was an immense disappointment. It was a home tie (good news) against Fourth Division Newport County (bad news). County had put Reading out of the Cup in 1951 and 1961 and were viewed as a hoodoo team. Given Reading's poor financial situation it was vital to beat them and progress to the 4th Round. Newport thought just the same thing for the same reason and 3,000 of their fans travelled to Elm Park. County, with a gale behind them, took a first-half lead. At change-round Reading benefited from the wind and went ahead with seven minutes to play. Then deep in injury time dismay as Gilbert Reece headed a shock equaliser at the Tilehurst End. The replay was just two days later but through forward planning by
94

the Supporters' Club's Mick Foster a special train had been booked and twelve packed railway coaches added to the crowd of 12,000 – Newport's largest in many years. It was a tight, hard game decided at the end by a clever through ball from Johnny Walker for Peter Shreeves to score. Walker described his part proudly and gleefully afterwards. The *Reading Chronicle* noted that on the way back to the station "the valleys echoed with a cheeky chorus of 'there'll always be an England' and 'REA-DING, REA-DING' as a column of blue and white clad fans walked the grimy streets of Newport".

League form had drifted away to such an extent that the focus was almost exclusively on the next round of the FA Cup for, at last, a First Division club was due to visit Elm Park. Burnley were not quite the heavyweight team they had been three years earlier but a mighty enough scalp to savour. "Enthusiasm has suddenly erupted in the town". The Saturday before the cup-tie Reading met Walsall at home, still missing Terry and Evans. Beforehand there was a demonstration by the RAF police dogs but even this failed to imbue a spirit of law and order. Always a bit of grudge match, this time it turned very nasty thanks to the "slackest display" of refereeing. Webb and Travers were injured by opponents and Wilkie was carried off. Reading lost to two disputable goals and a veritable riot ensued on the pitch at the end and in Norfolk Road afterwards as the Walsall coach came under attack.

There were hopes of a crowd of 25,000 for the Burnley tie but it was not made all-ticket. The club did not have any kind of system for selling scarce stand tickets. For the 2nd Round tie at Aldershot they had been arbitrarily put on sale at the end of a reserve match, to complaints, and for the Burnley game the 1,200 available stand tickets for home fans were at first sold on an unlimited basis before a ration of one per person was imposed. Hopes that many matches in the local leagues would be called off in order to boost the gate for the Burnley tie were dashed. In an unusually early nod to diversity a

Jamaican steel band was booked to play to the crowd before the game but unfortunately their sounds and timings clashed with the more traditional melodies of the George Watkins Band. In the event the attendance was only 17,872 and described as "pathetic in size and voice" by the *Reading Chronicle.*

One major extenuating factor for the numbers and the mood went unmentioned in the press: the match coincided with the state funeral of Sir Winston Churchill which had taken place that morning. After the service the funeral cortege made its dramatic, and televised, way from St Paul's, via the Thames and Waterloo Station and then by train to Bladon in Oxfordshire, actually passing through Reading about half an hour before kick-off.

A large part of the nation came to a standstill to pay their respects (for his distant relative Princess Diana's state funeral in 1997 all football matches were postponed) and looking at the timetable of events I can now see that I was among them, alongside my WRAF mum, rather than at Elm Park. I had gone to the Newport game on my own, aged nine, looking for and finding my friends in a 12,000 crowd and since wondered why I missed the Burnley tie. Such different times. However, I did get to hear some of the second half BBC radio commentary of the match, Reading's first time on the service.

Burnley took early control of the game. Andy Lochhead crocked Peter Kerr and then took advantage of him limping to score on 13 minutes.The Clarets then sat on their lead. Kerr was moved to centre-forward and on 75 minutes equalised with a low drive after a fine move to a tremendous roar. Reading pushed hard for a winner in the closing stages but it never came. At foggy, icy, Turf Moor in the replay Lochhead score the only goal five minutes from time. The Burnley supporters applauded Reading at the end and the team praised for the skill they had shown throughout the tie. Six FA

Cup matches watched by 82,000 fans had relieved the financial pressures.

But the energy of the team was spent. Hammered 1-5 in the Watford mud a few days later and sinking to 17th in the table, Reading were 13 points behind Hull and Gillingham, albeit with two games in hand. The smallest crowd of the season (5,164) greeted the team's return to Elm Park and were rewarded with the dullest game, a 1-0 win over Workington. Roger Ware in the *Reading Chronicle* wrote, "this lack of enthusiasm and spirit, except on special occasions, is worrying". Brian Sansome in the *Reading Standard* was more explicit. "People in towns with Third or Fourth Division sides are tired of bad soccer, of petty fouls and of promises seldom fulfilled. Poor accommodation, poor amenities and second-class players cannot be helped – but show some effort and provide value for money. Too many clubs seem to think that it's the public's duty to support them whatever brand of football they serve up". The threat was that "the drift to London" – and Chelsea specifically – would continue. Another impediment was the preference of many football enthusiasts for playing: there were 169 teams playing in the 12 divisions of the Reading & District League and the Reading Combination on Saturdays.

In March it was announced that Reading fans were to get their own social club and bar. "Nowadays you've got to offer something more than football. You have to be social-minded", said Fred May, moving towards the spirit of the times. He also put in for planning permission for four pylon floodlights (which were erected five years later).

Results continued to be infuriatingly inconsistent despite the returns of Terry and Evans. Reading drew at home with doomed Colchester then won at champions-elect Carlisle, lost to bottom club Port Vale, not trying to adapt to the ankle-deep mud, then beat league leaders Grimsby at home. Defeat at relegated Luton followed, then a victory over Mansfield that effectively denied the Stags promotion. Every week a coupon-buster, it seemed, but such triumphs seemed to frustrate as much as inspire. Against Grimsby the *Reading Chronicle* reported, "Dougie Webb had a nightmare match and how this often cruel Elm Park crowd let him know it. Maybe if Elm Park was to sound more like a football ground than a funeral parlour the Reading team might respond better than they do". A regular correspondent to the paper wrote back, "the club pleads poverty but surely there must be enough money to strengthen the team – let's face it, none of the directors are hard-up and if they're not prepared to back the club they shouldn't be there".

The season dribbled to a close with Reading losing their away games but winning their home games against higher-placed opponents. Youngsters Brian Knight and Ron Bayliss (who started the season in local park football) made their debuts. Evans was tried out at right back in place of Walker. Wheeler recovered from his broken leg to play four games and even Petts had a swansong appearance. Fairchild and Peter Knight, this season's new wingers, were notably absent. Meldrum was Player of the Season again, followed at some distance in the voting by Walker, Wilkie, Spiers and Terry. Wilkie had saved three penalties and was carried off injured three times. The final record was perfectly average – played 46, points 46, wins 16, draws 14, losses 16, goals for 70, goals against 70, position 13th – on goal average from 12th. There was a tight finish at the top, Carlisle taking the title by a point and Bristol City pipping Mansfield on goal average for the other promotion place with Hull and Brentford close behind.

Roy Bentley reflected, "there was not a good side in the division, no-one really worthy of going up by class". Reading, he must have felt and known, were as capable as these teams on their day but too many points were dropped to lowly teams through a lack of effort by players. His team took more points off the top four than the four relegated clubs. Bentley had had enough of trying to meld the new to the old, enough of giving the players a quieter life than he felt they deserved. His position had been strengthened by signing a five-year contract on better terms in the previous November. He announced that there would tougher discipline, training morning and afternoons and no more part-time jobs for players. It was well-known that Johnny Walker worked in a pub. His was by far the most significant name on the free transfer list – the once long-term captain, current assistant manager and favourite of a portion of the crowd. Walker hit back in the press, saying that at 36 he could still do a job and that "all the ball players had been sacked". Petts was finally given a free, the Scottish duo of Kerr and Grant, for whom it never really clicked, were gone too while Denis Allen and Ralph Norton were put up for sale. Wheeler was to take Walker's place as assistant manager and Spiers was to be captain with Meldrum dropping to vice-captain. Bentley was aiming for a more direct style and did his transfer business quickly in May, bringing in inside-forward Maurice Cook (Fulham), left-winger Terry McDonald (Leyton Orient) on free transfers and right-winger Alan Scarrott (Chippenham) for a small fee. Colin Meldrum and Arthur Wilkie responded by asking for transfers or bigger wages.

The financial picture had improved with the club, paying off some of the overdraft, making a profit of £6,000 and being helped by the Supporters' Club nearly doubling its donations to over £20,000. The 1965-66 season was going to be even more of a challenge for Bentley – but he was doing it more and more on his own terms and with a little more resource.

Meldrum scores against Fulham

Kerr scores against Burnley

READING
FOOTBALL CLUB

Season
1965-6

OFFICIAL PROGRAMME 6d

1965-66

- September – Evening Post launched to replace the weekly Reading Standard
- October - Emma Peel becomes part of The Avengers
- October – Brady and Hindley arrested for Moors Murders
- December – Sean Connery stars as James Bond in 'Thunderball'
- February - Swinging London and changing fashions
- March – Labour win General Election with increased majority
- June – Til Death Us Do Part (Alf Garnett) kicks off
- July – England win the World Cup

The changes in styles and fashions were gathering pace and the need to look beyond the shores of Britain was more pressing. The coming season was one of the most important in English football, culminating in the staging of the World Cup Finals. From the start of the season host clubs like Sheffield Wednesday and Manchester United were announcing how they had improved their facilities. United had spent over £300,000 on a new stand which included a restaurant and 34 private boxes to a provide a kind of 'Soccer-Ascot'. The football fan's eyes were drawn more towards Europe. West Ham had triumphed magnificently, live on TV, in the European Cup-Winners' Cup Final at Wembley in May 1965 while Liverpool were done down only by the referee in the semi-final of the European Cup.

The argument between the advocates of 'off-the-cuff' football and the 'well-drilled' approach continued to rage but the evidence was increasingly in favour of the latter. Yet an aged commentator decried the defensive game and expected the whole sport to die out by the end of the century! To illustrate the state of flux in football in 1965-66, whilst

Wednesday and United boasted of their modern facilities two of their First Division rivals (Sheffield United and Northampton) still played on cricket grounds.

Two developments symbolised the changing times. This was to be the first season that a substitute player was allowed in Football League matches but only to replace an injured player. The innovation depended on the integrity of the managers and was seen as quite controversial in that it (apparently) took some of the romance out of the game. The following season the rule was amended to allow a substitute to come on for any reason, the integrity of managers not quite coming up to scratch. Roy Bentley was scrupulous and only used four subs all season. Secondly, kit design moved in line with the style trends to junk the old-fashioned and the intricate in favour of the bold and plain. Liverpool, Chelsea, Bristol City and Cardiff were among the clubs that had moved to a one-colour strip (shirts, shorts, socks all the same). A change of kit reflected a change of outlook and Roy Bentley said, "new colours are a number one must, I want a new look all round next season (1965-66)". Without much ado it was decided that Reading would abandon the blue-and-white hoops worn, almost continuously, since 1938 in favour of an all sky-blue strip, thus imitating those soccer pioneers of Coventry City. The *Reading Chronicle* published a vox-pop survey and some fans agreed that the hoops were "outdated", or that "anything would be an improvement" while just as many felt they were "smart" or "distinctive". Around Reading there appeared some curious, very modern, yellow and black 'Op Art' posters. This was the 'teaser' campaign for the launch of the *(Reading) Evening Post,* the town's first-ever daily newspaper. It significantly increased the coverage and therefore the interest in the club.

Bentley and the Board knew they faced strong challenges. The previous season average gates in the Third Division were down by an alarming 18%, the worst in the League. Reading were halfway down the Third Division attendance table too. So, it was back to Plan B – Friday night football in the warmer months - in the hope of attracting some of the 2,000 amateur footballers thought to be in the town. That would be a tough challenge; one letter writer said, "there are people in this town who enjoy watching amateur soccer ... and have little or no interest in professional sport, if it can be called sport". The floodlighting was improved with the addition of 24 lamps. The Supporters' Club Social Club in the stand was opened, at an additional subscription of ten shillings.

And for the first time in several years there were some genuine local derbies on the fixture list. Swindon had been relegated from Division Two and Oxford United had been promoted from Division Four in only their second league season. Suddenly local pride was at stake. Historically Reading had held the upper hand over Swindon but that had changed in the past five years while Oxford United had been less of a feature than the once popular Oxford City. However, crowds at the Manor were now slightly in excess of those at Elm Park. For Reading fans there was a sense of local pride needing to be restored. The press seized on the potential of these rivalries, what in later years would be known as the Didcot Triangle, and gave the derby matches the full cup-tie style treatment.

Yet despite all these challenges Bentley contrived to go into the season short-handed. After the flurry of signings at the end of May (Cook, McDonald, Scarrott) he stated he wanted a squad of 24 players. But he started the season with just 20, which included youngsters Ron Bayliss and Brian Knight with just four appearances between them and veteran / assistant-manager Jimmy Wheeler. What did he think was going to improve the team? The sky-blue kit? The absence of Walker? More discipline? Harder training? For this, his third, season he would look around the dressing room and see the same old faces – Maurice, Dick, Arthur, Denis, Dougie, Rod, Mick,

Peter, Ralph, Gordon, Jimmy Wee – all pals there before he arrived, all tried and tested, part of over 30 away defeats in the last two and a half seasons. Bentley could point to Colin Meldrum, coming to his peak and thankfully unsold during the summer, and potentially a new forward line – Scarrott and McDonald either side of the belligerent Pat Terry and the crafty Maurice Cook. But there was not much back-up.

Heavy-spending Hull City were the clear favourites to win the division in both *Football Monthly* and the *Reading Chronicle* and the latter was the far better tipster as regards the rest, picking Millwall and Swindon to be among chasing pack. Reading, reasonably enough, were not mentioned.

Sometimes the first game of the season is strangely indicative of the 45 to follow and this was one such occasion. On 21 August a very decent crowd of nearly 12,000 came to see the debut of the sky-blue shirts. The opponents were the dour and brutal Watford. Reading began with their usual 20 minute blitz towards the Town End. Pat Terry opened the scoring and there could have been more. Just before the break Watford equalised when a shot was deflected past the unsighted Wilkie. Reading were back on top when Peter Shreeves was clobbered and Ralph Norton became the club's first ever substitute. He didn't get in the game and Watford scored again with a long shot that left Wilkie "puzzled". "The Watford rear-guard was content to kick anything that moved", claimed the *Reading Chronicle.* Reading tired and there was no further score. After his League debut Alan Scarrott said, "it took me some time to get used to the pace. I enjoyed it but I didn't think much of getting kicked almost every time I got possession. I suppose that's the way they play in this division".

Scarrott was the only one of the three new men to make any impact on the season. He was 20, still single and living in digs, and had spent time with both West Bromwich and Bristol Rovers. He offered an uncannily accurate delivery of crosses and corners for Pat Terry to feast upon. His youth and lack of

105

physicality contributed to significant inconsistencies in his performances but he did make 33 appearances. The far more experienced newcomer on the other flank, Terry McDonald, was another busted flush of a winger, just 13 appearances including a sending off for dissent. Roy Bentley didn't even pick his other new signing for the first game and Maurice Cook made just 12 appearances in the league. Two out of the three signings were failures and no new men were signed during the season despite the long pursuit of forward Dave Metchick of Orient. It was a case of new shirts, same players, and what the *Reading Chronicle* dubbed "a sky-blue disaster" on the first day.

Reading did not win until the fifth game by which time Wilkie, who had worn the green jersey for the best part of two and half seasons, was dropped in favour of Mike Dixon. By the end of October Reading were a point off the bottom and a place above the relegation line. By the end of November Millwall and Hull were well clear of the rest and occupied the two promotion places for the rest of the season. Reading were 11 points behind but with games in hand. There was never a promotion challenge but the games in hand were persistent. It took until 19 February for Reading to start their second half (i.e. 24th match) of their League programme, a landmark normally reached in mid-December. They finished with seven games to play in May and 14 points short of the runners-up spot.

The Elm Park crowd was as restless, frustrated, disappointed and angry as ever. Foul play and poor refereeing contributed to the mood. When Mansfield punched their goal into the Reading net the crowd came on the pitch to confront referee Rex Spittle and a bottle was thrown. A few weeks later a heavy metal plate from the half-time score-board was thrown at the referee and the FA ordered the club to post warning notices around the ground. In January the club banned two boys for persistently throwing toilet rolls and other litter.

Reading were continually the victims of late equalisers – or failing to close the game out, depending on your point of view. Gillingham – "a crude apology for a football team" (*Reading Chronicle*) – were one of the beneficiaries, having battered Fairchild and McDonald all game long. Their manager Freddie Cox was to Reading fans in the Sixties what Neil Warnock became in the Noughties and he told the newspaper, "blow the crowd. I don't care tuppence about entertaining the crowd so long as my team wins matches".

Football crowds were changing in nature. They were becoming more youthful but also more disruptive. There was cross-over with the pop culture and the use or adaptation of hit songs into terrace anthems – 'you'll never walk alone' being the prime example. This anthem may have started and finished in Liverpool but every club in the Sixties sang it as a favourite. The crowds in general were making more noise and the players took encouragement from this. Singing and chanting made going to football more interesting and participative, especially at away matches. At the same time there was a trend to heavier pre-match drinking (more money, less Saturday morning work). The popularity of Match of the Day and its focus on the big city clubs created new norms of what was expected from a football crowd in the provinces.

Roy Bentley knew from first-hand experience of visitors at Elm Park that this was another area where Reading were lacking and together with the Supporters' Club set about tackling it. He thought, "the whole Coventry set-up is so fantastic that enthusiasm alone could get them promoted (from Division Two)" and that he had heard, "many years ago the Elm Park Roar was a well-known asset to the club". He wanted non-stop cheering from the word go from under the clock to the counter the voices of visiting supporters. Brentford were said to have an "organised cheer squad" told to rally in that exact same spot for the FA Cup-tie. Millwall, of course, took it to a whole new level, letting off fireworks from under the clock, abusing the minute's silence in memory of a Supporters' Club official, starting scuffles in the stands and terraces, invading the pitch at the end and kicking Pat Terry (their former player), before damaging the train on the way home. But they did give "first-class vocal support". So too did the 3,000 Swindon supporters: "the Robins' choir made Reading's so-called supporters look pretty pathetic" said the *Reading Chronicle*. The retort came by letter the following week – "never have so many been let down by so few. We expect 100% effort and we don't get it". By the end of the season there were plans to formalise "a cheer club" under the clock for the next season to try and change the unsupportive mood on the terraces.

The results of the four derby matches against Swindon and Oxford were an immense disappointment for supporters. Yet again Reading had won praise in faraway places – the best team to visit early pace-setters Grimsby, robbed of victory at powerful Hull by a "diabolical piece of officiating" and believed by the *Reading Chronicle* that "when they put their minds to it they can beat anyone in this wide-open division". But when it came to the "most vital game" it was a different story. The first ever league meeting between Reading and Oxford United drew a crowd of almost 20,000 to Elm Park, the highest home league attendance of the Bentley era. It was billed as the "big neighbouring brothers" against "the Southern League side who grew up". Oxford were a well-drilled lot who had played together for some years, enjoying success in the Southern League, the Fourth Division and reaching the FA Cup quarter-finals. Nevertheless, they were perhaps under-estimated by the Reading public. They out-fought Reading who "stumbled ineptly, aimlessly to defeat" – a Mick Travers own goal early in the second half deciding the game.

A month later a heavily re-jigged team, trying to cope with the dropped Spiers, travelled to the County Ground, Swindon. Roy Bentley, desperate to do some transfer business and as always unwilling to sign a player he had not personally watched, missed the game to go scouting. Over a thousand Reading fans went by special train or coach to witness a thrashing. Meldrum was switched to the right flank to counter Don Rogers but the Swindon winger scored a second half hat-trick in a 5-0 romp. Spiers was put straight back in the team for the rest of the season but McDonald hardly played again.

Reading's visit to The Manor in late March was billed as 'Revenge Day'. It would be "a complete loss of pride" if the Biscuitmen were defeated. Two thousand fans travelled in support to give the game a cup-tie atmosphere. There was much petty fouling and some fighting in the stands as Reading went down tamely by two goals to nil. Bentley said, "I completely lost my head with them at half-time". The *Reading Chronicle* noted that Oxford had sold two players and bought two players in at a net spend of £13,000. The final derby game was at home to Swindon on April Fools' Day. Reading were playing their fifth game in ten days and Don Rogers scored the only two goals. Four derbies, four defeats, no goals scored, ten conceded. Disappointed fans picked up their pens again. "The forward line is non-existent. The directors must dig deep into their bank books. Everyone is fed up with Third Division football and seeing the same teams year after year".

The frustration of these results was compounded by the change in form generally between November and March as Reading climbed the table and did well again in the FA Cup, benefiting from three home ties in a row. Third Division rivals Bristol Rovers (3-2) and Brentford (5-0) were beaten with the reward of a 3rd Round match against First Division Sheffield Wednesday. After the messy handling of the Burnley game this tie was rather better organised. It was made all-ticket and even Oxford United were involved in the selling efforts. The Supporters' Club again sold trackside seats (the last time this facility was ever used) and with the *Reading Chronicle* helped put together a programme of recorded music to draw

109

spectators in early. Among the songs you could request were 'we can work it out', 'you need hands' and, topically, 'World Cup Willie'. There was a souvenir programme and the *Reading Chronicle* commented, "such enterprise from a club which does not hold public relations as high as it should do on its list of priorities is to be applauded". Bert Eggo and John Hunter who had played in the 1929 victory over Wednesday were invited as special guests. The club's reward was an attendance of 22,488 and a good, tight game. When Maurice Evans made it 2-2 near the end it looked as if another lucrative replay was in the offing. But in the final moment Mike Dixon's error coming off his line allowed Johnny Fantham to score a lucky winner off his ear. The League Cup had brought a modicum of glory through beating Second Division Derby County in the 3rd Round before a dismal 1-5 exit at Cardiff in the next.

The two remaining highlights of the season were the matches against the obvious promotion contenders, Millwall and Hull. Hopes of 20,000 crowds did not materialise. The game against Millwall was described as "a real he-man affair" with Alex Stepney denying Reading until a late equaliser from Scarrott. Hull won comfortably by the only goal on a Friday night on their way to points total of 69 – the highest in this era.

Thereafter it was a case of getting through a crowded and compressed fixture list. Bentley could afford to give a few youngsters a chance – Peter Silvester, Ron Bayliss, Brian Faulkes and Ian Maidment. The surfeit of football – five home matches and two testimonials in May alone – saw attendances fall below 5,000. Poor Maurice Evans' testimonial at the end of this run attracted less than 2,000 despite the attractions of John and Mel Charles, Maurice Edelston and Roy Bentley all on the pitch.

For there was another local rival grabbing the attention, a very local rival that by the end of the season was drawing more

110

support than Reading. Jimmy Wheeler's Reserves team was chasing promotion to the Football Combination Division One.

It was clear from October that they had a chance and they started to draw four-figure crowds. Wheeler was out of the first team but still a popular figure and the Reserves were "just as entertaining if not more so than the first team" in the eyes of the *Reading Chronicle*. The temper of the support might be judged by the fact that fans at the Reserves game actually cheered when it was announced the first team were losing badly away at Cardiff. The Reserves principal rival for the one promotion place was Gillingham.

At end of January they hoaxed Reading by sending their first team, unannounced, in place of their reserves to Elm Park and won 3-2. Even the neutral *Football Monthly* called Gillingham "dour and defensive" and this act of deceit confirmed the impression that they were one of the more unpleasant clubs in the division. It made the promotion contest even more important.

In March Reading Reserves beat the leaders QPR with over 2,000 watching. Bentley wanted their promotion because he expected the higher standard would improve technique and performance, making players ready for the first team more quickly. Moreover, the home club kept all the gate receipts and that could enable the Reserves to pay their own way. Their success was good for the morale of the whole club at a difficult time. By mid-April the Reserves were top of the table and the Supporters' Club were running coaches to their away games.

The words 'promotion favourites' were like catnip to the Reading faithful – whatever the league or standard. It came down to the final game, at home to Bournemouth (now managed by Freddie Cox), a point was needed to win the title.

Over 6,000 came and, in an electric atmosphere, it was gained. The swarm of kids under the clock cheered frantically and invaded the pitch in their hundreds at the end as free fights broke out between a few players. It might only have been the

Triumphant Jimmy Wheeler with fans young and old

Football Combination Division Two but it was a promotion at last, the first for 40 years. It showed that success would win over "the very hard hearts on the terraces". It must have been quite odd for Roy Bentley to look on at all this enthusiasm for a team built out of his rejects that was outdoing his own efforts. To mark this accomplishment for all time the supporters voted Jimmy Wheeler Player of the Season – and it was obviously not because of his mere two first team appearances.

From the first team perspective it had been rather a waste of a season, though the fans had nine cup-ties to enjoy. The club was well aware that just standing still in effect was a licence for slow decline. Towards the end of April the *Reading Chronicle* headlined a story "All Systems Go for Division Two" and stated, "Reading Football Club shook itself out of its self-imposed slumber which has lost public interest for so many years". There were at last profits to be spent and Roger Ware estimated a transfer budget of £25-30,000 available for two good class players and a much-needed facelift for Elm Park. Roy Bentley boldly claimed, "this is the real thing, not another fairy story" and that the club were now willing to spend up to £15,000 on a player. In a way the story of 1965-66 had been the failure to buy, to strengthen the team at all during the season. Bentley had been ultra-careful, the club were nervous of the new and expensive trend on signing-on fees and also put off dipping into the non-league market by 'shamateurism' – the illicit payments made to so-called amateur players. Giving a strong hint about the retained list to come Bentley said he wanted "a tricky, brave winger who can tough it out in Division Three".

The retained list was a bonfire of wingers. Out went Mike Fairchild, Peter Knight, Brian Knight and Terry McDonald, failures one and all. Also on the list were Ralph Norton and Peter Shreeves, two inside-forwards of the old school who had never firmly held down a place, Maurice Cook, a one season flop upfront and poor, injured, Gordon Neate who would continue to serve the club well into the next century as groundsman. The youngsters showed the way ahead, winning at Exeter with "eleven men willing to chase endlessly". The combination of little transfer activity, slightly increased gate receipts and donations of over £17,000 from the Supporters' Club created a profit of £8,000 and enabled a further reduction of the overdraft.

And so to the 'Summer of '66' which it has to be said felt rather different in late July to mid-May. There was not much sense of World Cup build-up in Reading though Smith's Coaches did advertise trips, ticket included, to France v Mexico at Wembley and also to a pre-tournament friendly between England and Jugoslavia (sic). The nation was in a miserable state caused by financial crisis and a major docks strike. The lead into the tournament began with an Ealing

113

comedy moment as the World Cup trophy was stolen from a stamp exhibition but recovered by a mongrel which found it under a bush. For England's opening game against Uruguay there were several thousand unsold tickets and the team was booed off after a 0-0 draw. The hard hearts weren't just at Elm Park. Astonishingly only eleven matches were televised live, with the focus being on England and Brazil so the tournament wasn't quite as gripping as might be imagined. England made it through the group stage but the main talking point had been the abrasive play of Nobby Stiles. If England had gone out in the quarter-final to Argentina, as seemed quite possible, it would all have been a damp squib. But those last eight days transformed English football history: 1-0 against the ten men of Argentina, 2-1 against Eusebio's Portugal, and then the Final that England famously won twice against West Germany.

I was eleven years old and in no fit state to judge. James Bond was clearly the world's best secret agent, the Beatles were obviously the world's best pop group so it was in the natural order of things, as far as I could see, that England were now indisputably the best football nation having won the World Cup. Football was the game, Ty-Phoo was the tea with all the promotional colour team pictures and rosettes you could collect and Subbuteo table football filled the spare time. Even though they were just ten minutes' walk away Roy Bentley's Reading didn't bleep very loudly on my soccer radar now.

Terry and Evans fly in against Millwall

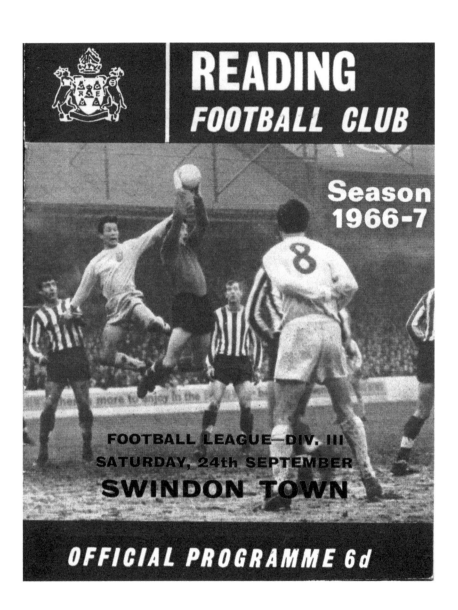

READING
FOOTBALL CLUB

Season
1966-7

FOOTBALL LEAGUE—DIV. III
SATURDAY, 24th SEPTEMBER
SWINDON TOWN

OFFICIAL PROGRAMME 6d

1966-67

- October – Aberfan disaster as coal tip collapses killing over 100 children
- November – Cathy Come Home TV play / launch of Shelter homeless charity
- March – Torrey Canyon oil spillage, major environmental disaster
- April – 100-1 Compton-trained Foinavon wins Grand National
- June – Beatles' era-changing Sergeant Pepper album

Of the six seasons of his management the closest Roy Bentley came, mathematically speaking, to achieving promotion was 1966-67. To be utterly precise, one more goal against Middlesbrough on 18 March would have been just enough, when the tables were finally calculated, to achieve that long-desired aim. Yet two weeks after that game the *Reading Chronicle* mused on 31 March that "Reading could yet find themselves in an unexpected relegation struggle". However at 4.40pm on the last Saturday of the season Reading occupied the second promotion place, following victory at Workington watched by a handful of away supporters. But 53 points was never going to be enough. Watford picked up a point from a 3.15pm kick-off and then Middlesbrough won their game in hand the following midweek to clinch that second spot behind QPR, the only strong team in the division. The *Reading Chronicle* described the effort as "nearly how to succeed in the promotion race without really trying" and "more accident than design". Reading had finished a dark, dramatic, fractious, crisis-ridden season with eight consecutive wins. Unfortunately, they had needed ten in a row.

The season opened in a spirit of optimism, determination and innovation; all systems go, remember! George Harris was signed from Watford as a striker / winger, John Chapman from

Workington as a defender and Ron Foster from Grimsby as a midfielder for fees totalling about £12,000. There was a new club entrance and offices and a new staircase for the directors. The Supporters' Club funded the introduction of tip-up seats to replace benches in D Stand and over the next two years that benefit was extended to the other four stands. The Social Club was now open three nights a week. The Blue Streaks youth section for fans 14-21 was launched as a 'cheer group' and a one hour pre-match recorded music programme replaced the traditional band music.

The opening match was lost 0-3 in sweltering heat at Torquay and an early injury crisis saw veterans Jimmy Wheeler and Maurice Evans in the full-back shirts. For the fifth game versus QPR Colin Meldrum and Dave Bacuzzi, just signed on a free transfer from Manchester City, took their places and there was a brief revival. "Reading never cease to amaze me", wrote the *Reading Mercury*, "they handed out a merciless soccer lesson to highly-rated QPR for an hour then ruined everyone's afternoon by allowing Rangers the luxury of a point". Accusations of lack of fitness and lack of effort, especially among the forwards, abounded in the press. Bentley himself issued a reprimand in the programme: "it is obvious far more effort and determination is needed in order to win matches. Players must surely realise we as a club are judged on results". There was short-lived relief when Reading beat Swindon 2-1 at Elm Park in front of less than 10,000 (if the gate had been bigger would they have been put off?) and followed it up with a 3-1 win at Oxford. "Lords of the Manor" yelled the headline accompanied by pictures of Reading fans waving banners in the London Road end. Headed goals by Pat Terry from Alan Scarrott crosses were making all the difference – along with new men Bacuzzi, Foster and Harris. Roger Ware thought, "they will never have a better chance of promotion".

But then the wheels just fell off, precipitating a storm of protest, an absolute crisis and the brutal termination of several long Reading careers in the space of six weeks. At the end of this period Bentley was both somehow stronger and weaker; stronger because he'd at last destroyed the old pals' nest in the dressing room and got something more like the younger, stronger, fitter team he wanted; weaker just because the dressing room was now his alone and he was one excuse fewer from the end.

The crisis began, as often in those times, with an anaemic-looking October home fixture. "With 30 seconds left to play Colchester were allowed to literally stroll through and score the winner. Not one reasonable tackle was made in the move that led to the goal", wrote the *Reading Chronicle*. Roger Ware followed this up with a piece demanding "new players before it's too late" and attacking the club's (Bentley and the directors) inertia in the transfer market. The club dismissed the article as "a stab in the back" but the readers were with the reporter. Reading took just two points from the next seven games as the crowds plummeted from 7,000 to 4,000. Judging from those figures and the correspondence columns the mood was spectacularly ugly, so much so that one wonders if grim national events played a part. In these self-same weeks there was a wage and price freeze, sudden and large rises in unemployment, a national man-hunt for Harry Roberts who shot and murdered three policemen in cold-blood in London, the heart-rending Cathy Come Home TV play about homelessness, Alf Garnett's splenetic rantings on the air-waves, the Aberfan disaster in which over a hundred children died when a coal-tip slid and engulfed their school, followed the next day by the escape from Wormwood Scrubs of George Blake, a notorious Soviet spy. These were some of the darkest days of the Sixties and lashing out about any kind of misery was a little more understandable.

Amongst the complaints of the Elm Park faithful were the painfully slow efforts in the transfer market, the complacency of the club and directors, the lack of a qualified trainer / coach to get the players fit, directors "hiding in their shells", boring football, Bentley being too lenient with the non-triers, "too many faint hearts" and a feeling that "Reading has for too many seasons enjoyed a reputation as the finest rest home in professional football".

The most cogent and wide-ranging critique came from a supporter of 45 years standing. He thought, "in a nutshell the club is woefully short of talent, spirit and direction... the second and third deficiencies can only be made good by sound management". His reforms would include appointing a high-profile player-manager such as Dave Mackay (then of Tottenham), building a team of 90-minute triers, removing the secretary (Fred May) and placing his duties of "in the hands of a retired person of the executive type who possesses a forceful personality, a distinct leaning towards Press liaison and the ability to sell Reading Football Club to an apathetic public". Squadron-Leader Ayres, the letter writer, then posed two rhetorical questions of the directors – are you getting 100% effort from your employees and are you giving the club the necessary backing?

Other supporters pointed the finger more directly at the directors. "Do the directors really think they can get promotion with a team of cast-offs?" "The present board of directors should make way for a more progressive body." "There are too few new directors". As if answering these calls on demand the *Reading Chronicle* ran a front-page story about Ron Blindell, a vice-president of the club and 'a shoe magnate', who offered his services as a director. He was turned down flat by Frank Waller (vice-chairman) who said, quite disingenuously, we have "a full quota of directors" but would consider Blindell "if and when a vacancy arose". It was, of course, completely within the board's power to create new directorships as they

120

had done some years previously. Blindell did have a reputation as something of a dictator and might have been a man worth avoiding. He had been chairman of Plymouth Argyle in the late 1950s and was ousted there by his own directors! Following Waller's rebuff Blindell turned his attention to Griffin Park and put up the money (largely as a loan) to save Brentford from being taken over by QPR in January 1967. A year later he sought to relocate Brentford to Hillingdon and rename the club Brentford Borough. Whilst Blindell might have livened things up at Elm Park it might well not have been for the better.

Prompted by the lowest home league crowd since the war (4,111) for the goal-less draw with Bournemouth the crisis came to a head. Chairman Alf Smith announced, "the present team is not good enough". In an unprecedented move Reading effectively sacked five players. Technically they were put on the transfer list and left to rot in reserve team football. The five were youngsters Ian Maidment and Brian Faulkes and the established names of Mick Travers, Dougie Webb and, most surprising of all, Maurice Evans. Webb (aged 27) and Evans (30) were certainly not seen as being amongst the "non-triers" and were valued by many supporters as "good club men" with more than 600 appearances between them. But to Bentley they were the tried and tested past, unlikely to ever improve their game. This was not just the end for Evans, Webb and Travers. Jimmy Wheeler would never play in the first team again either, Gordon Neate was retired through injury and became the groundsman, Mike Dixon was replaced by Arthur Wilkie for the rest of the season and Dick Spiers was dropped for four months. Roy Bentley had effectively ousted the old guard of local boys in the Elm Park dressing room. Then he went to Crystal Palace and bought Ernie Yard to replace Maurice Evans in his midfield.

The first test of his new-look side was at home to Grimsby on 16 November. Reading were four up at half-time and added two more even after Pat Terry was sent off. The *Reading*

Chronicle said, "this was the first real show of spirit and enthusiasm Reading have produced this season" and commented on the vastly improved, younger, half-back line of Ernie Yard, Ray Dean and John Chapman, the unspoken comparison being with the likes of Evans, Spiers and Travers. The 6-0 win was greeted with chants of "easy, easy" from under the clock. At last Bentley had found a formula as Reading now won six matches on the trot. He was vindicated. The 3-1 win at promotion-seeking Oldham was judged "the best performance in a decade" and Reading were labelled in the press as "Bentley's Battlers". The team at Oldham was Wilkie; Bacuzzi, Dean, Chapman, Meldrum; Yard, Thornhill; Scarrott, Allen, Terry, Harris. The fans came back with over 10,000 watching the Boxing Day revenge match against Walsall. Two more wins and then Reading visited League leaders, the "all-conquering" QPR. They were the best Third Division team of the era. They won the division by 12 points and also became the first club from this level to win a national cup competition by defeating West Bromwich at Wembley in the League Cup final. The following year QPR were promoted into Division One. Their side was a mix of expensive experience in Les Allen, Rodney Marsh and Jim Langley and exciting youth in the Morgan wing-twins and Frank Sibley. At Loftus Road Reading missed early chances then fought back from two down to have a chance of equalising with a late penalty. George Harris put it over the bar but over the two games home and away Reading could show they were a match for the division's best.

There was also another FA Cup tie at the Aldershot's Recreation Ground in the offing, just two days later. Reading's re-vamped team had made easy meat of non-league Hendon in the 1st Round. With a 2nd Round tie offering the prospect of an attractive draw in the 3rd Round there was more at stake and more needle in this local derby than there had been in the 1964-65 1st Round match. On form Reading were firm favourites. There had been a fair degree of gamesmanship beforehand in arranging the match. For the original date the Shots' Dick Renwick would have been suspended and Pat Terry eligible to play, thanks to Bentley pulling "a fast one" and asking for a personal hearing for his star centre-forward. People in Aldershot felt Reading were trying to cheat. When the match was postponed for a second time, with the pitch implausibly described "as virtually under water", Reading folk felt Aldershot had deliberately watered the pitch so that the game would be played when Renwick's suspension was over and Terry's had begun. The 3rd Round draw had come up with Brighton at home as the reward for the winners – a winnable tie from Reading's point of view. The local papers gave the match the usual big cup-tie treatment and all was set for a dramatic night at the Rec.

The game was finally played on a cold Monday evening. An estimated 6,000 Reading fans travelled but the traffic around Aldershot was horrendous. Crowd control at the ground was hopeless as a record 16,500 turned up with more locked outside, some climbing the surrounding trees to get a view, some breaking down the gates to get in. Many of those inside the ground couldn't see a thing because the crowd was too tightly packed at the bottom end while there were spaces at the top covered end. Fans clambered up floodlights and onto the roofs of stands where they fought a running battle with police. Reading began casually, Aldershot fiercely. Reading were knocked out of their stride and, arguably offside, Jack Howarth scored the only goal early in the second half. Reading pushed hard at the end, Denis Allen hit the post, but without Terry upfront they went home bitterly disappointed – and considerably out of pocket given the money that would have come from a replay and a 3rd Round tie. "In terms of prestige Reading have dropped the biggest brick for a long, long time", said the *Reading Chronicle.*

Whilst QPR looked nailed on for the top spot the runners-up slot was wide open and fast-improving Reading could close the gap with good results against three local rivals in the next three games. However, "Watford's method men poached a point" at Elm Park where the continued absence of Pat Terry meant the home side could not convert their superiority into anything more than a 1-1 draw. He was back for the visit to Swindon who had just knocked West Ham out of the FA Cup. Over 3,000 Reading fans, banners aloft, travelled on a sunny afternoon. "Swindon were outfought and outclassed by a Reading side that was as near perfect as makes no odds", glowed the *Reading Chronicle*. George Harris lashed in the winner in the 48th minute as Reading moved up to 8th and the Robins fell into the relegation places. The victory brought Reading the official Football League 'team of the week' award and supporters were licking their lips at the prospect of lowly Oxford's visit to Elm Park. Another win would give the Biscuitmen a clean sweep of four out of four in this season's Didcot Triangle derbies. The *Reading Chronicle* mixed bullishness with caution. "There is little doubt that on man-for-man ability Reading are superior, vastly superior, and on form should win". But it also recognised Oxford's desire for revenge, need for points and the big home crowd jinx. Bentley was confident: "if we play as well as we did at Swindon ... we should win without too much trouble".

Nearly 14,000 watched Oxford's "methodical sort of kick and rush backed up with 100% determination" out-fight Reading in what the *Reading Chronicle* called "their best effort at public suicide for some time. In its timing this defeat was yet another disaster in a generally disastrous season". Terry gave the home side a half-time lead but the visitors were allowed back in and won 2-1 with a late goal. Two away defeats followed and Reading were now in the bottom half, four points from the relegation places and 14 points behind second place. With the season looking to be over the Board took the

124

surprising step of selling attack leader Pat Terry to relegation-threatened rivals Swindon for a fee quoted as £8,000 (actually more like £5,000).

Peter Silvester had been flourishing in the Reserves and had been joined there by 18 year-old Roger Smee, a promising local boy returning home after time at Chelsea. Both were candidates to replace Terry if Bentley couldn't buy before the deadline. Pat Terry had been a very strong player and character in the team, perhaps too much the focus of the attack, but he was a "have boots, will travel" striker who hadn't settled locally. The move worked for Swindon who rose to finish 8th just three points behind Reading.

Roger Smee scored in his first three games, the third of these at Middlesbrough on 18 March. This wasn't a fixture that looked as if it would decide the promotion race but at 2-2 late on Reading missed two great chances. As it turned out eventually that would have made the difference but no-one could possibly have guessed. Easter brought Reading the usual poor fare, just three of the six points available, and raised concerns about relegation in what was a very tight division. Dick Spiers and Ron Foster came back into the team which then played more or less unchanged to the end of the season.

There were eight games to play when Leyton Orient came to town to play on a bumpy and dusty Elm Park pitch, a 7.30pm Saturday kick-off to avoid clashing with the Grand National. Harris scored the only goal and established a club record for goals scored by a winger. The rest of the fixture list wasn't at all demanding and Reading won all eight, keeping six consecutive clean sheets. The *Reading Chronicle* commented, "it's a long time since Reading had a recognisable system and even longer since they had one that worked." Roy Bentley had the freedom to experiment and the strength to impose a 4-2-4 system which he aimed to have played rigidly throughout all the club's teams down to the

125

Minors. In what may be a coincidence Denis Allen asked for a transfer again and was listed at £5,500. As the season came to a close, Foinavon making his circuit of Elm Park, the frustration of being so close, of starting this winning run just too late, was painful. "Oh, for three more points", wrote Roger Ware in the *Reading Chronicle*, "it sickens me to think of the drawn games that could have been won and the defeats that could have been draws … the ironic thing is that as recently as March Reading officially gave up the ghost and sufficient points have gone down the drain without seeming to matter … just a few months ago it was decided to let the first team drift on as best they could with a concentrated effort of saving the Reserves from relegation". Bentley flatly denied that last claim. Despite some good results towards the end the Reserves did indeed go down. The first team finished their home programme in style with a "glittering display" full of "purpose and skill" against Oldham. So it all went to the last game. Reading needed to win at relegated Workington, Watford to lose at Oldham and Middlesbrough to drop one point from their last two home matches. At rain-swept Borough Park, in front of a mere 856, Reading won 2-1 and heard that Watford were behind at Oldham. But Watford equalised and then Middlesbrough went on to overtake them and return straight back to Division Two.

Reading were left with the regrets of starting late – if only results from mid-November had counted they would have been promoted – and hopes that at last Bentley had found the formula for success and the men he could trust to try all the way next season. It had been billed as the 'All Systems Go' season and, to bear with the metaphor, it stalled on take-off, he changed half the crew and then just missed the target by two points despite that late burst of acceleration. Nine away wins was a big improvement. George Harris, with 25 goals from left wing, won Player of the Season with Meldrum and Yard second and third. The retained list was as expected from
126

the November coup. Mick Travers joined his old friend Ron Tindall at Portsmouth while Maurice Evans considered offers from Aldershot and Hillingdon but eventually went to Andover.

On the terraces success brought some calmness, though the referee needed a police escort after inexplicably denying Reading a late winner against Mansfield. There were few reports of hooliganism, some good and vociferous away followings and noise from the Blue Streaks at home. Even the letter writers set aside their green ink for a while. Gate receipts were slightly down (fewer cup matches) at £50,000 but the club still turned a small profit of £3,490. The switch back from Friday nights to Saturday afternoons had made no real difference. At the August AGM chairman Alf Smith whiningly contrasted the lowest average gate since the war (6,927) with missing promotion by a point (it was two, in fact) though winning the last nine (it was eight) games to reach 55 points (it was 53) – and failing to mention anything of the mid-season crisis and criticism. His inaccurate report showed something of the attitude of mind and the sloppiness of the directors and secretary/manager.

The Supporters' Club had a tremendous season and donated over £30,000. Their Giant Jackpot scheme was almost at its maximum of 15,000 members and a new match day bingo ticket was devised with the proceeds to go to a new, far larger, social club. The call went out for "24 pretty girls" who were clearly thought to have a better chance of separating the gnarled and overwhelmingly male regulars from their shillings. It was not a ground-breaking idea; Bristol Rovers already had their "True Blue Trudys" selling their bingo tickets. The premium on attractiveness went both ways; every issue of *Football League Review* soon contained a table of the most attractive players as nominated by thousands of signatures collected largely by young women in thrall to the charms of George Best, Emlyn Hughes and the like. Supporters from out of town railed against the Town End social club proposal as being just for Reading-based folk and would have preferred the money spent on covered accommodation behind the goals. In the event neither element got what they wanted and nor were they much enthused by the summer concert with Freddie and the Dreamers at Elm Park after the Beatles' Sergeant Pepper album hit the shops.

What had changed was the feeling that Roy Bentley had finally got the playing pieces in place, that there was a genuine transfer budget available, that the heat was off the directors, that the club was beginning to make progress off the pitch and that Reading should not fear any side in the division next season. Eight wins on the bounce and still counting ….

Harris scores against Swindon

Reading fans enjoying the game at The Manor Ground

READING
FOOTBALL CLUB - OFFICIAL PROGRAMME 6ᴰ

FOOTBALL LEAGUE DIV. III   SATURDAY, 14th OCTOBER, 1967

BURY

SEASON 1967/68

1967-68

- July – colour TV launched in UK
- September – 'The Prisoner' series begins on TV
- November - De Gaulle vetoes UK bid to join Common Market
- November – the pound devalued in financial crisis
- January – 'I'm Backing Britain' campaign launched to counter national pessimism
- March – sterling crisis, run on the pound; huge tax rises
- March – peace march and riot in Grosvenor Square
- April – Thames Valley Police formed to replace local forces
- April – Enoch Powell's 'Rivers of Blood' speech and subsequent sacking

If any season was to be the season this was to be the season. In a way it was; some great results, just not always in the right competitions. It was Roy Bentley's fifth full season and hopefully the execution of that five-year plan, not that there had been much evidence of a steady progression. Nevertheless, the *Reading Chronicle* considered these to be Reading's best prospects in the past ten years.

Before the start of the season two new forwards were added to the squad. Big, bustling John Sainty was a replacement for Pat Terry. At 21 he was yet to make his League debut but he'd had a good career so far in Spurs' Reserves and he'd cost the substantial fee of £12,000. John Collins was an experienced forward signed from Oldham for £7,000 and knew the division well, also from his time with QPR. By Reading's standards these were major investments. Reserve keeper Mike Dixon decided to go part-time and run a newsagents, otherwise there were no changes to the squad. So determined was Roy Bentley to impress the 4-2-4 system on players, press and public alike that he abandoned the traditional shirt-numbering system. Now numbers 3 and 4 were centre-backs, midfield at 6 and 7 and the wingers were 8 and 11. The *Reading Chronicle* announced, "for the first time in years there is a real club spirit among the playing staff at Elm Park" which makes one wonder what had gone unsaid in the years before. To further that spirit Roger Ware suggested (perhaps briefed by the players?) that there should be a first team squad of 16 all to be paid first team money which would be £10 per week more than reserve team wages.

There were still financial pressures. The playing staff was cut and trainer Bill Lacey made redundant. Admission charges were raised by a shilling all round, the first increase in seat prices since 1960 and terrace prices since 1964. At five shillings the price of an afternoon's football was compared to a gallon of petrol or two pints of beer. However, there was good news for old age pensioners who would be admitted at half-price if they showed their pension-books at the under-15s gate. All part of a policy of "shaking off the heads in the sand attitude which has held the club back for some time", commented the *Reading Chronicle.* Indeed, the club went so far towards innovation they were reprimanded by the Football League for setting up an unauthorised pre-season tournament also involving Oxford, Aldershot and Brentford. Yet there were still problems with national journalists that led Roger Ware to comment, "for too many years the public and the press have been regarded almost as unnecessary evils at Elm Park". Fred May kept a tight rein on press and photographer passes, hence the almost complete absence of colour action images from Elm Park, the front cover of this book being a singular exception. Reading joined 71 of the other 92 League clubs by including the *Football League Review* magazine in the match day programme but Roy Bentley ceased to pen the first page – and the style suggests Roger Ware might be doing this too.

Unseasonal heavy rain greeted the opening day of the season. Stockport County, the champions of the Fourth Division, were the visitors and they brought a large contingent of supporters on a special 'Bingo Train'. They started several nasty fights in Elm Park in what was probably the first occasion of mass hooliganism in the ground. I blame the Bingo! John Sainty scored twice on debut as Reading won 3-0. With crowds at the 10,000 mark three more games were won (including Bristol Rovers in the League Cup) taking the sequence of victories to twelve.

The 13th game was both notorious and tragic, a real turning point. Shrewsbury were another club long stuck in the Third Division who fancied their chances of getting out this season. They were known as an aggressive outfit and they went for Reading from the first whistle. Reading, now with a record to protect, fought back in kind and referee Laing (Preston) lost control. Colin Meldrum was concussed in the first half, had stitches in a head wound and had to spend the night in hospital. The referee cautioned him *after* the game for something said when he was in a befuddled state. Shrewsbury took a two-nil lead with a penalty and a fluke. Ernie Yard was sent off in a skirmish and would later be suspended for three games, all of which were lost. Dave Bacuzzi had his leg broken and would effectively be out for nearly four months. George Harris pulled a late goal back but the aftermath of this defeat to close rivals would linger for months. The Supporters' Club said "it left a nasty taste in the mouth". Roy Bentley was furious: "I do think the referee should have clamped down on several players in the Shrewsbury side, one in particular who went over the ball in almost every tackle".

Two games later came perhaps Bentley's finest moment as Reading manager – a 3-1 victory over First Division West Bromwich Albion in front of almost 19,000 at Elm Park in the League Cup 2nd Round. It was a thrilling match in a tremendous atmosphere as Reading ran themselves into the ground but were skillful enough to make it look like a clash between two First Division sides. "When the final whistle blew Reading's sweat-stained heroes were buried under a deluge of delight", gushed the *Reading Chronicle*, noting the huge pitch invasion at the end. Harris had scored twice and Arthur Wilke was brilliant in goal. Next up in the 3rd Round was Reading's first ever visit to Highbury to play Arsenal.

Tired and a little distracted Reading could only draw at Elm Park to Walsall the following Saturday, old adversary referee Spittle denying the home side a late, clear, penalty. The standard of refereeing generally was still a cause for concern with Denis Allen critical in *Elm Park News* and Leslie Vernon in *World Soccer* stating, "British refs are the worst in the world, the biggest bunch of homers I will ever have the misfortune to meet". Despite some mixed results Reading were still third in the table when Swindon visited. Nearly 18,000 packed the ground and once more Reading didn't disappoint, fighting hard, playing well and shading it by two goals to one, "a glorious night for a makeshift team". The derby games always seemed to come in pairs so three days later it was a trip to The Manor. Bentley thought afterwards Oxford were "the worst team we have met this season". Reading missed chances, went 2-0 down and gently subsided. Referee Lewis (Port Talbot – and years later a greater thorn in Reading's side) baffled the crowd with his decisions and strangely announced over the loudspeaker that he would abandon the game "if certain sections of the crowd did not cease using bad language". This was something Reading fans had picked up from a recent visit to Swindon!

Midweek saw the League Cup tie at Arsenal. Cup fever raged in Berkshire with 10,000 travelling up to London but traffic congestion meant that the majority didn't enter Highbury until after half-time. Reading were already one down but produced a barnstorming second-half show, roared on by the now much-enlarged away support. They hit the woodwork twice and had a goal disallowed but couldn't find an equaliser. Bentley called it "the best performance by the team since I arrived". Reading fans were enjoying the taste of big-time football but it was back to Elm Park for a vital Third Division match.

Bury were in the close, and large, pack chasing Reading who were now fourth. Bury's history and present strategy were almost the opposites of Reading's. They'd won the FA Cup twice, way back, and they'd only recently ever dropped below Division Two. In all probability (educated guess here) they were one of the clubs that continually voted against expanding the number of promotion places from Divisions Three (North) and (South) which for so long held back clubs like Reading whilst protecting their own position. Far better connected to the heartlands of football they had decided to spend their way out of Division Three. In their forward line were two ex-First Division men, Alex Dawson and Ray Parry, but their real gem was Bobby Collins. Aged 37 the former skipper of Revie's Leeds was still an immense driving force and he was reputed to be on £100 a week, probably three times the wage of most Reading players, and probably worth it. Bury were to do the double over Reading. If that had been the other way around it would have been Reading, not Bury, who got promotion.

In retrospect this match was a vital turning point. I didn't see it but I remember the result as a surprise and recall fans walking past our front garden cursing about it on the way back to town. Rain, gale force winds and a subdued home side. It went 1-0, 1-1, 1-2, 2-2, 2-3, 3-3 and with a minute to go 3-4. Bobby Collins had run the show and Bury had pressed a tiring team right until the end. Colin Meldrum now began his unjust 14 days suspension for words uttered to the referee when concussed and Ernie Yard joined him on the banned list. Reading went to Swindon without either and also the injured Sainty. Arthur Wilkie, who had been playing exceptionally well up to the Bury game, had another nightmare as Swindon won

135

5-1 with Pat Terry scoring twice. The *Reading Chronicle* saw this and the loss at Bournemouth as "the official exit of Reading as promotion runners" – by the end of October and as per usual.

For all the gung-ho words at the start of the season and the praise received for several brilliant performances all was not well in the dressing room. Ron Foster and Roger Smee put in transfer requests in September. They had been crucial parts of the winning run at the end of the previous season but were now out of the team and on reserve wages. The form of the wingers Alan Scarrott and George Harris had dipped. Their obvious replacement Jimmy Mullen was surprisingly sold after a first team career lasting just eight games, simply because a good fee was offered. Sainty and Bacuzzi were injured, Meldrum and Yard grated on their suspensions and Wilkie was peremptorily axed from the first team for the rest of the season. With youngsters Ray Dean and Ron Bayliss in the back four the need for more solidity meant abandoning 4-2-4 for a 4-3-3 line-up. By Christmas Reading had sunk into mid-table and normal service had sadly been resumed.

There were two bright lights. The Division Three promotion race was still wide open; there were no outstanding teams of the calibre of QPR or Hull City. And the FA Cup. For the third time in four seasons Reading had drawn Aldershot. This time the tie was at Elm Park and this time there was no messing around. Well, there was a postponement due to snow but in the mud and mist four days later Reading showed little mercy. They were five-up at half-time, six with 20 minutes to go before allowing the Shots two goals and the chance to miss a penalty. Many Aldershot fans had begged to be let out of the ground at half-time. It took a tough replay to overcome Dagenham in the next round (Reading were "unpopular winners") and secure a tie at title-chasing Manchester City.

Truly these were days of milk and money for the board – three First Division sides in the same season and this to be

136

the biggest gate of the lot, over 40,000. Two special trains went from Reading, fare £2. Spurs were playing at United on the same afternoon and the City and United yobs combined to harass the travelling southerners at the station. City were complacent and Reading were nervous and attacked very little. City were awarded a 'home town' penalty near the end which Tony Coleman skied over the bar and Reading had an unexpected home replay from a goal-less draw.

Over 6,000 people queued hours, most of them pointlessly, for the 1,000 stand tickets available and sold from a single counter. Fred May responded to the criticism, "obviously in such a situation we will come under fire whatever we do. We will, I think, try and devise a new method next time". Roger Ware advocated programme tokens which in fact were adopted in 1972. The solution suggested by the Supporters' Club was – buy a season ticket. A crowd of 25,659 came to watch. They had a treat, but not the one they wanted. City had been given a rocket by Joe Mercer and Malcolm Allison and came out all guns blazing. Reading were overwhelmed by their skill, speed and power. The *Reading Chronicle* summed it up in the headline "OH, OH, SEVEN!" City won by a scarcely credible (well, I didn't believe it at first) 7-0, apparently a national record home defeat in an FA Cup replay. Bentley gave the team the day off to forget about it and they responded with a win with a new man on the wing.

It was three months since Mullen had been sold and Scarrott was no longer featuring. Bentley's search for another winger was as prolonged as usual but, armed with Cup cash, he settled on, judging by newspaper speculation, his fifth choice – John Docherty from Fourth Division Brentford at the rather expensive price of £12,000. Docherty held down a place, Bacuzzi and Dick Spiers were back, Sainty was more or less fit and when he wasn't Smee or Silvester stepped in. But the results were an uninspiring mixed bag and the attendances declined to 5,000, a sign that the public knew that

137

the season was more or less up given there was, surprisingly, no more transfer activity.

AREFF's graphic take in the Reading Chronicle on the 0-7 Cup defeat

Yet it wasn't quite. On 30 March with 10 games to go Reading were 6th just four points behind Bury in 2nd place and a point behind Oxford who were 5th. The leaders Torquay were a fragile point ahead of Bury. A late burst like last season's effort could see Reading win promotion from an indifferent division. On the menu were mid-table Peterborough. They brought a massed defence, an offside trap and stole the game with a soft goal. Reading were again "the masters of the anti-climax" and the 4-2-4 system was rubbished in some quarters as too negative. It was Bury and Oxford who got their skates on as Torquay cracked. Reading dented Watford's hopes with an impressive 2-0 home win and with six to play still had a slight chance. But then they lost at Barrow, at Southport and at home to Oldham, all games they should have won on the balance of play. This last defeat set the disappointed crowd off on a spree of barracking, breaking the corner flags and hurling stones at the dressing room windows. This drew a harsh and angry response from Bentley, calling them the worst supporters he'd ever come across. To emphasise their inconsistency Reading then won the last three games including a 4-0 thumping of the long-time leaders, Torquay.

Oxford took 20 from the last 24 points and the title; Reading took 14 and finished six points behind Oxford, five behind runners-up Bury, back in 5th place. The frustration was immense. Not only had Reading blown their best chance in years but the prize had gone to a local rival who were judged, locally it should be said, not to be worthy of it. Not only had Reading been inconsistent, both brilliant and awful, but they had come close enough at the end to feel that the prize had been in reach all along. This was a team that had beaten the FA Cup winners (West Brom) and drawn away to the League champions (Manchester City) but flopped against no-mark Third Division outfits with nothing to play for. The *Reading Chronicle* sympathised with Bentley: "to have assembled the goods and not got the required degree of success must be terribly frustrating for him".

For the penultimate home game against Scunthorpe the crowd was down to another post-war low of 3,739 and the bitter, accusatory letters arrived at the local press. Fans were arguing again with the man on the loudspeaker: "stop trying to deceive us you men at Elm Park. We are sick of those pathetic remarks". Another raised the old trope of the club not wanting to go up because of increased wages and costs. A third added, "truly most supporters are fed up with years of dreary Third Division kick and rush. London and the big clubs are in easy range of most of us and TV whets the appetite". Manchester United had made their heavy mark on the public consciousness by winning the European Cup at Wembley in late May.

Several of the players had had enough too. Colin Meldrum, still the mainstay of the defence, asked for a transfer. So too did Ron Bayliss and Peter Silvester. The latter request was turned down. Allen, Thornhill and Foster were already on the list though the first two then came off it.

139

Bacuzzi, Harris and Smee ended the season out of contract while Bentley decided that Alan Scarrott's league career was over. He was given a free transfer to Hereford. Arthur Wilkie's position was quite uncertain. He'd been tried out in the Reserves as a forward (he did, and still does, hold the record for most goals scored in a league match for a player who started the game in goal) but at the relatively young age of 25 opted for part-time non-league football which seemed a waste of a talent. Unsurprisingly both Jimmy Wheeler (now 35) and Dougie Webb (29 but injured all season) hung up their boots. All in all it would seem that the dressing room had lost faith in the five-year plan or the wages they were being paid for what was not a bad season.

A year later Bentley, reflecting on his whole reign, said of 1967-68 "it all looked set but certain players didn't re-capture their form and then we were crippled with injuries. The whole lot folded up and we were never in with a serious chance". Mike Dixon was the Player of the Season with George Harris, Denis Allen and Colin Meldrum also in the running. Harris again led the goal-scoring charts with 27 in all competitions. John Sainty's total of 12 from 34 games was a slightly disappointing return for the big fee. The football club accounts showed a loss of £1,500. Gate receipts were up at £65,000 and the Supporters' Club chipped in £29,000. There was an unusually high net spend on transfers of about £23,000 (Sainty, Collins, Docherty in, Mullen out). Overall the financial and playing strength of the club looked to have improved but the surrounding morale and atmosphere did not reflect that.

At a black- tie event at the end of the season Fred May was presented with a gold watch and Frank Waller with a silver salver, each for 20 years' service to the club.

Supporters were left wondering quite where the club went from here. Would it be the same forever? "We appeal for your continued support although promotion once again seems to have slipped away ... I can assure supporters that the
140

Directors and Management always strive for promotion" were the plaintive messages from the Supporters' Club. It felt like something was ending. Credibility, perhaps?

Alf Smith presents Fred May with an award. Frank Waller, far right

Some of the 3,739 watching the match against Scunthorpe

One of the six of the best against Aldershot

Collins scores against Scunthorpe

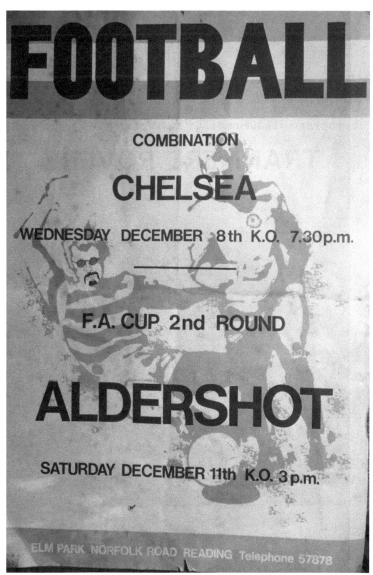

Match poster from 1967, amended in the style of the day

READING
FOOTBALL CLUB - OFFICIAL PROGRAMME 9ᴰ
(INCORPORATING FOOTBALL LEAGUE REVIEW)

FOOTBALL LEAGUE DIV. III　　**SATURDAY, 14th DECEMBER, 1968**

TRANMERE ROVERS

SEASON 1968/69

1968-69

- July – 250,000 attend Rolling Stones free concert in Hyde Park
- August – 'Dad's Army' appears on TV for first time
- November – more austerity and cuts: Government massively unpopular
- November – last trolley bus journey in Reading
- January – widescale rioting and violence in Northern Ireland
- February – strike at Ford factory presages year of industrial unrest
- March – Yoko Ono 'joins' the Beatles – the end of the band is nigh
- March – first flight of Concorde

If you could say the Sixties didn't really get going until the middle of 1963 you could just as well say the energy, the optimism, the spirit of all-togetherness of the Sixties really began to fade by the middle of 1968. Even the patriotic 'I'm Backing Britain' campaign was attacked by unions who didn't want to see workers working for nothing. The spring of 1968 brought student unrest onto the streets, massive riots in Paris and the controversy over Enoch Powell's 'rivers of blood' speech. In Reading a large swath of the town centre was a waste land while the Inner Distribution Road was built. The failure to complete the M4 ensured huge traffic tail-backs and it could take motorists an hour and a half to cross town on the jammed A4. The Mansion House in the centre of Prospect Park was a decaying derelict ruin. The shabbiness and disconnectedness of Reading irked some who felt the bright lights of the Sixties were passing them by. A group of Caversham Park Village residents hit the front page of the *Reading Chronicle* in March with their claim that "Reading must be the deadest, dullest, most boring, 'dragsville' with the powers and dignity of a County Borough". Bar billiards leagues obviously not good enough for them. No wonder that suburb soon acquired, according to urban legend, the reputation as a hot-bed of wife-swapping. In the wider world it was a time of anger, violence and uncertainty: the Vietnam war, the assassinations of Robert Kennedy and Martin Luther King, the Soviet invasion of Czechoslovakia and race riots in the USA.

At Elm Park the summer was, by contrast, worryingly quiet, except on Wednesdays when the players came back for enforced, unpopular, close season training sessions. Jimmy Wheeler had taken up the offer of the manager's job at Fourth Division Bradford City. Ron Bayliss went with him and together they achieved promotion in their first season. Wheeler's desk at Elm Park remained unoccupied for four months as Roy Bentley did without an assistant. The much sought-after Dave Mackay was now about to work his miracles for Brian Clough at Derby.

Alf Smith stepped down as Chairman of the club at the August AGM. He had served five years and was now aged 74. He was succeeded by his vice-chairman, naturally, Frank Waller, he of the bushy white moustache and uneasy smile. Waller was to hold his new position for the next 15 years, making 30 years in total on the board, at the end of which he would try to extinguish the club in a so-called merger with Robert Maxwell's Oxford United. But in 1968 he had ambitions that a more business-like approach to running Reading FC would pay dividends. He was also conscious that Roy Bentley was entering the last full season of the five-year contract that he signed in November 1964. Waller stated, "we want promotion – and quickly". There was no new director appointed in place of Smith so the Board was now just four strong. Waller, with his chairman's casting vote and pal Leslie Davies alongside, was more or less in complete control.

It was well-known that there was a transfer budget of around £25-30,000 to be spent in strengthening what was now

146

a very small playing staff of 17. Ron Foster had left to join Dallas Tornado. Paul Bence signed on a free from Brighton but the only buy Roy Bentley made was Spurs' reserve goalkeeper Roy Brown for £5,000. The effective size of the squad was reduced further when Roger Smee broke his ankle in the first minute of the first pre-season friendly and Mike Dixon broke his arm. Smee came back only for the last game while Dixon never played in the first team again.

The decline in attendances for League matches towards the end of the previous season had been a worry so Reading decided to go back to playing matches in the warmer months on Friday nights. In this they may have been encouraged by the example of Southend whose Friday night gates were up by 3,000 which they put down to shop staff and amateur footballers being able to attend and Saturdays becoming a more 'family' day. In general League football was booming with gates back above the 30 million mark but Division Three was suffering. The boom at the turnstiles contrasted with the criticism that football was getting in the press: hooliganism, dirty play, poor facilities, awful refereeing but there was clearly also plenty of excitement and personality in the game at the top level. Reading retrenched further by abandoning their Minors side and moving the 'A' team from the Hampshire League to the South East Counties League.

The sense of energy and enthusiasm draining away was present elsewhere. The Supporters' Club ceased publication of Elm Park News, didn't organise a New Year's Eve dance (the Monday night bingo sessions in the Huntley & Palmers canteen had long gone) and no longer provided commentaries on away games in the social club. In the New Year its two fund-raising schemes were scrapped in favour of one super-scheme as Jim Brooks took over the chairman's role there. The *Reading Chronicle* was slighter and sketchier on its pre-season preview, offering the opinion that Reading "would find it tougher than last year" and upholding its reputation as tipster by picking out Watford ("will make few friends"), Swindon, Luton ("big financial backing") – the top three as it happened – plus Tommy Docherty's (short-lived) Rotherham. Later in the year the paper didn't send a reporter to some distant away games.

Elm Park might have been quiet and withdrawn but over the summer a new noise could be heard further down the Oxford Road – the Reading Racers speedway team set up at the Greyhound Stadium by Scours Lane. The *Reading Chronicle* treated the Racers with the same status as the football club and soon the Racers were drawing crowds of 6,000 in British Speedway League Division Two. The promoter Reg Fearman was an accomplished publicist and Roger Ware drew the obvious contrast: "when it comes to public relations the speedway people win hands down. Reg Fearman treat the Press like gold dust". By the end of their first season (1968) a supporters' club had been set up to organise away travel and a fan claimed "the speedway crowd are far more loyal than the football crowd" – though of course there was a fair degree of cross-over. Reading Racers had a freshness and dynamism that Elm Park was striving to emulate.

The first big game of the football season was a dull 0-0 at Swindon. An unusually pragmatic Bentley came with a 4-3-3 and for a draw. It was a different story next against Hartlepool, a home win by 7-0 with new golden boy Peter Silvester scoring four. With seven points from six games a crowd of nearly 12,000 was encouraged to Elm Park for the clash with long-term rivals Watford on a fine Friday evening. Even I went. Watford came for a point, frustrated Reading and the crowd and stole both points with a late goal from a corner. I can remember the disgruntlement around me on the Tilehurst End. The seven goals against Hartlepool might as well have been a mirage. This, sadly, was the real deal. "Big Game, Big Flop". But with 11 games gone Reading were back in the chasing pack, fifth, three points off the top, visitors Swindon a point

148

behind. It was the ideal opportunity to prove the Watford defeat was a mistake. The *Reading Chronicle* anticipated a crowd of 20,000. In the event only 17,000 watched a poor game decided in the Robins' favour by a scrambled first half goal. "Oh No, Reading, not again!" read the headline. Victory would have put Reading second but this defeat was the prelude to the usual autumn slide. After the game 150 fans fought outside the station. By the end of October Reading were mid-table while Swindon, Watford and Luton were the top three which is where they stayed. After a first half against Brighton, described as "pathetic and laughable" the crowd raised a tremendous cheer when the referee blew the whistle for half-time. The barrage of complaint from supporters on the terrace and in the papers intensified. One correspondent described himself as "an avid soccer-hater and in particular an avid Reading soccer-hater" but then his script descended into furious illegibility!

Orient scored in the first minute, Reading failed to do so from 21 shots and cries of "Bentley Out" came from under the clock. Roy Bentley wasn't there to hear them. For the third first team game in a row he was elsewhere scouting and mulling over his transfer budget. Ray Henderson, formerly of Hull City, had been appointed player-coach a month earlier (mid-October) and felt enough at ease in his new job to say to the press, "these people make me sick, they have no idea of the difficulties". With Smee and Sainty injured Meldrum was put upfront while Bentley hunted for another centre-forward to answer his problems. He offered £15,000 for Frank Large, the patron saint of "have boots, will travel" strikers. But even Frank wouldn't travel to Elm Park. Another military man caused a furore in the letters' column. Major McDonald abandoned the cause in late September thus: "from me it's good-bye to Reading FC for the rest of the season. I'm off to London for my football. It happens every year".

He took his aim at the directors, "pseudo football-loving businessmen" and demanded "a lot of re-thinking" from them. He even had a word for the Elm Park faithful, "the brave, obstinate people who deserve a little more from the club". Tongue possibly in cheek he wrote again a fortnight later to apologise for any offence caused, saying he had visited Elm Park once again and remarked that the "lack of effort is so utterly apparent". Reading in fact won 3-2 and the Major was obviously a hard man to please but he found some support for his views and analysis.

Reading's home form was decent enough but they didn't win away between September and April. Consequently, they were the usual five or six points behind the leaders and lurking down in mid-table as Christmas came. On an icy cold afternoon Reading beat Tranmere 2-0 on a rock-hard pitch in front of another new low post-war attendance of 3,250. Christmas shopping called more loudly. The FA Cup offered some consolation. Reading were drawn at home first to Plymouth, then to Torquay, both clubs near them in the league table. Success in both ties took them to the opposite end of the country in the 3rd Round – St James' Park, Newcastle, one of Roy Bentley's old haunts. There was less enthusiasm for this trip. The special train left at 7am and cost £3.10s. The 400 supporters were intimidated the moment they got off the train and spread themselves voicelessly among the 41,210. Bentley decided to back the experience of Docherty and Spiers and so dropped Sainty and Dean. It was an unpopular move that didn't pay off. Newcastle were a shade lucky to be 2-0 up at half-time and two more late goals flattered them. "There was never four goals in it", said Bentley. He had another purpose in the north-east that weekend – to sign Newcastle's veteran defender Jim Iley as his 'Dave Mackay-type' classy, inspirational figure to shake-up his team. He thought he had him in the bag but on the Monday Iley announced he had a better offer to become player-manager at

Peterborough. Out of the Cup, way off the promotion pace and unable to spend his transfer chest this change of mind from a vital potential recruit must have been a sickening blow for Bentley. For the fans he had become part of the problem, not part of the solution. The 'cheer group' had lost faith in him, especially his slow and non-existent transfer dealings. "Other managers sign lots of players. Come on Reading, pull yourselves together. The supporters need glory. They look around and see Oxford in the Second Division, Swindon at Wembley and heading for the Second Division too. Give us something to cheer or the crowds will get smaller and smaller" wrote one.

Bentley was desperate, flying around like an agitated bumble-bee searching for a forward to buy. He missed the home game against Southport and the away game at Orient. Henderson must have been in charge but what kind of authority would he have over the likes of Spiers, Allen and Meldrum. The speculation kept coming. Harkin of Shrewsbury? Andrews of Southport? Greenhalgh of Villa? Or why not his colleague Woodward? The word must have got out that Bentley was on borrowed time. No-one would sign. He decided on Yeo of Gillingham and agreed a price of £15,000 which was £5,000 more than he publicly admitted the player was worth but said the decision was up to the Board. If the Board didn't back him the *Reading Chronicle* diplomatically reported, "it would raise an extremely delicate situation internally".

Bentley watched a Reading Reserves side containing several first team regulars lose at Fulham on 5 February and blew his top afterwards. "The lack of effort in some quarters was appalling. It makes you wonder if some of them are interested in anything but taking home their pay-packet". They were probably more interested in who the next manager would be and when he would appear for it was clear he had lost the dressing room, the terraces and had issued, essentially, a

151

'back me or sack me' message to the Board. On Monday 10 February he was summoned to Frank Waller's office in Sonning and, in a quite gentlemanly way, fired. The club would pay up the last nine months of his contract. Waller expressed regret at not having longer than a year to work with him (what had he be been doing as vice-chairman?) and said, "he was a first-class man. We never interfered in any way". Bentley, for his part in the immediate aftermath, replied, "I have no grouse against the club and the directors and couldn't have wished for better support". In a probably more honest vein he told Roger Ware he accepted the decision with "a sense of relief" and put his failure down to "a lack of consistency, a deficiency he couldn't put a reason to". Bentley's emollient words about the Reading club and directors (but not, note, players and supporters) were those of a man who would like a manager's job elsewhere. In August 1969 he was appointed manager of Fourth Division Swansea City and said, "one of my main reasons for accepting the post was that I was impressed by the enthusiasm that obviously existed in the club and which, unlike many clubs, started at boardroom level". Is it fair to dwell for a moment on those last eight words? Roy Bentley achieved promotion in his first season as Swansea manager.

Reading's 1968-69 season still had 18 games to run and caretaker-manager Ray Henderson wanted the job on a full-time basis. He scrapped some of Bentley's tactics and reliance on formations, went back to the traditional shirt numbering formula and demanded no slacking from the players. They won the first home game 4-2 against Stockport and there is the oddest team photo taken before the game by flash in the cramped dressing room. It appeared in *Football League Review* and shows a rather glum set of footballers (see back cover). Henderson and the players soon fell out; he called some of them "totally unprofessional". The season dragged on. The *Reading Chronicle* had a nice line about "a Reading side which now only plays because the Football League says
152

it must" – less than 3,500 at Elm Park for that one. The results weren't terrible but it was a matter of playing out time before the new man was appointed.

Supporter Tony Bampton wrote in to demand a 'Reading Revival' campaign when the new man arrived. Bampton's demands were for a return to blue-and-white hoops, the appointment of a PR man, an improved programme, new floodlights, an electronic scoreboard, a new social club (all of which happened and most within a year!) and spookily re-naming the club Reading Royals FC. I must ask Tony when I next see him (he's still a season-ticket holder) who put him up to all this. It's certainly the first mention made of the vapid and overblown nickname that the club adopted soon after the Huntley & Palmers biscuit factory closed in 1976.

The search was taking time in part because "Reading are handicapped by being an honest club" unwilling to use subterfuge to approach managers currently in work. After Ronnie Allen decided he'd prefer Bilbao to Berkshire Jack Mansell became the firm favourite and was appointed on 14 April. There's something of a tradition in the new manager being in many respects the opposite of the old manager and in this case that certainly applied. The ways in which Mansell was different from Bentley shed some light on Bentley's shortcomings. Bentley was hewn purely out of post-war English soccer: Dubbin, Brylcreem, chain-smoker, man's man, tell it like it is stuff but deferential to directors. Mansell was three years younger so he just missed serving in the war. He was with Manchester United as a youth and had a not particularly illustrious playing career with Portsmouth, Brighton and Cardiff. But he had seen the world of football outside England, managing two Dutch clubs, a spell coaching at Ajax, a qualification as an FA Staff coach and arrived at Elm Park fresh from Boston Beacons, one of the first wave of soccer clubs in the USA. He had also managed Rotherham in Division Two for a short time. So, unlike Harry Johnston or Roy

Bentley, he was no insular rookie as a manager. Compared with Bentley's now somewhat tousle-haired, haggard, sheepskin jacket image Mansell was clean-cut and sharply-dressed in the mould of a young American senator (Robert Kennedy comes to mind). According to the *Reading Chronicle* he "came in like a force ten gale blowing away many of the smaller cobwebs from the Elm Park set-up". He instantly removed the TV and radio from the dressing room and demanded and got his own office and personal secretary rather than share with Fred May as Bentley had done. He insisted on a return to blue and white hoops, saying it was "a distinctive colour scheme that gave Reading an image of its own". The new four-pylon floodlights were to go up in the close season as he set about altering the club's image, working on a new youth scheme and building a scouting network. The *Reading Chronicle* portrayed him as a master of tactics, strict disciplinarian, utterly self-confident and well aware of the value of public relations and stood him in contrast to the "antiquated, watch-every-penny set-up at Elm Park". The report on his first match in charge suggested "Reading played it much closer than they have been doing" and a couple of games later they were playing "the push and run stuff" (aka the one touch football) with which fans became familiar the following season. He had three games to experiment with, all lost by a single goal as Reading fell from 11th to finish 14th in the table, 21 points shy of the two promoted clubs, Watford and Swindon.

Swindon's story was the more famous as they emulated QPR by both winning promotion from Division Three and the League Cup in the same season (it's never been done since). The Robins beat Arsenal in a memorable mud-spattered Wembley final the day after Reading had lost at home to Plymouth in front of just 5,000 – just to make the galling comparison. Actually, for the most part Reading applauded them as old friends and fellow provincial underdogs. It would be a decade before Swindon – and Oxford – returned to

154

Reading's orbit. Watford's story was more ordinary and more painful for that. Ironically it was Watford's approach to Roy Bentley that resulted in Reading giving him a five-year contract in November 1964. Roger Ware spent a few paragraphs analysing their success, with the help of some inside information, and he didn't need to make the comparison with Reading explicit. Watford had a superb defence, they played an unattractive 4-5-1 formation, they conducted an intricate analysis of the opposition in order to neutralise their threats, they were prepared to attack late on in away games to snatch undeserved winners - as they did at Elm Park, they gave 100% effort in every game because their fiery boss, Ken Furphy, would not tolerate less. Thus they achieved success with "mediocre players", conceding only 34 goals in 46 games and winning ten matches by 1-0. Dedication on and off the pitch. It was their first ever promotion to Division Two since joining the League in 1920 and the 21,000 who came to celebrate a 1-0 home win over Jack Mansell's Reading on 19 May weren't that bothered with the quality of football on offer.

Danny Williams, the Swindon manager, observed, "Division Three is probably the most difficult of all in which to play football. Too many sides seem intent on using brute force rather than skill, making It difficult for young players". Roger Ware's take on Roy Bentley's team was that, "when it comes to the rough stuff Reading have always lacked subtlety. There are sides that kick lumps out of anything that moves but they do it under the counter where only a hawk-eyed referee can spot it". Reading were not trained or programmed in the dark arts and defenders like John Chapman, Dick Spiers and Colin Meldrum were caught out when resorting to their own initiative and departing from Bentley's "sound constructive football".

In the end of season honours Peter Silvester won Player of the Season from Roy Brown and Denis Allen. Silvester was second top scorer with 16, one behind John Collins. In order to get to know his new men better Jack Mansell ordered two

155

weeks *post-season* training, morning *and* afternoon, at Bisham Abbey, at the end of which he decided on the retained list. Mike Dixon, Ray Dean and John Chapman were given free transfers and Ernie Yard and Rod Thornhill made open to offers.

Financially the club had made a miniscule profit of £800 even though gate receipts were down by about 20% and the Supporters' Club contribution by a similar proportion, at £25,000. In a way it's amazing that the Supporters' Club lottery efforts held up so well when the all-around interest in the club was draining away. The 1968-69 season, and in particular the spring of 1969, represented the transition from the homely time of Smith-Bentley-May to the more business-like era of Waller-Mansell-May-and a marketing man. A year earlier the York City chairman Mr Bundy stated "there is no longer any time for those directors who regard the job as merely a pleasant form of relaxation". In the same publication, *Football League Review,* Bryon Butler wrote, in November 1968, "it is a fact that some Boards are not equal to the task of making a success of their clubs. Their club may have achieved nothing for two decades. Teams and managers have come and gone; the only common denominator is the Board of Directors. They may have done their best but that is not always enough. It is certainly not enough in the harsher world of commerce". There would be many Reading supporters, including doubtless the hard-hitting, letter-writing military duo of Squadron-Leader Ayres and Major McDonald, nodding at those words.

Storton (Tranmere,5) scores an own goal at a near empty Elm Park

The bare facts

Div III	P	W	D	L	W	D	L	F	A	Pts	Pos
1963-64	46	15	5	3	6	5	12	79	64	52	6th
1964-65	46	12	8	3	4	6	13	70	70	46	13th
1965-66	46	13	5	5	6	8	9	72	63	51	8th
1966-67	46	13	7	3	9	2	12	76	57	53	4th
1967-68	46	15	5	3	6	4	13	70	60	51	5th
1968-69	46	13	3	7	2	10	11	69	66	43	14th

	Avge gate	Top scorer	Player of the season	Promoted clubs
1963-64	8,434	Webb (14)	Colin Meldrum	Coventry (60) Palace (60)
1964-65	7,533	Webb (18)	Colin Meldrum	Carlisle (60) Bristol C (59)
1965-66	8,857	Terry (23)	Jimmy Wheeler	Hull C (69) Millwall (65)
1966-67	7,119	Harris (25)	George Harris	QPR (67) Middlesbrough (55)
1967-68	8,127	Harris (27)	Mike Dixon	Oxford U (57) Bury (56)
1968-69	6,552	Collins (17)	Peter Silvester	Watford (64) Swindon (64)

158

The reckoning

How close did Roy Bentley come to achieving his promotion goal? The bare facts of the league table are there for all to see but they don't tell the full story. There was never a moment in the second half of any season where a supporter could think 'this is ours to lose now'. Sure, there was potential, as there was at half a dozen other Third Division clubs too, but it was never really close despite finishing 4th, 5th, 6th and 8th. The expectation peaked in 1967-68 and after that failure it was a matter of him playing out time. Six years nowadays seems a long time to be the manager of a club that just stands still.

In some respects Bentley was a little idealistic, naïve, too kind. He managed Reading as if it was someone else's club, as if it belonged to the directors or the long-serving players. He didn't create his own environment and he didn't adapt enthusiastically to the way football was changing in the Sixties. He wanted to play 4-2-4 and tried to make the players fit the system rather than the other way around. His selections and tactics didn't often adjust to the opposition or the conditions, too often caught out trying to pass through ankle-deep mud. He never once brought in a player on loan, he hardly used substitutes, he rarely disciplined players, he was too cautious in the transfer market and he wouldn't go down the route of dirty, defensive play. He was as much with the players as above them. On the way back from an away victory they were all having a boisterous meal together in a hotel. The owner came to Roy to reprimand him and he said, "I'm sorry, sir, but these lads are all trainee monks and this is their last night out before going into the monastery". Old supporters still say of him 'he was a gentleman' and that in a way is a reward. He also worked tremendously hard with not a lot of resource in terms of managerial assistance, especially after Jimmy Wheeler left, and when the heat of the moment had passed people remembered him with affection and respect. This would not be the last time Reading FC employed his talents.

Would another manager have succeeded? The next three managers (Mansell, Charlie Hurley, Maurice Evans) didn't achieve promotion from Division Three either. As it took a wholesale revolution in the club 20 years later before genuine progress was made, perhaps we have to look elsewhere for the reasons the club just stood still?

Reading FC in the Sixties needed mould-breaking in both senses of the word. It was not just stuck in a mouldy, decaying pre-Sixties' past; it was also stuck in its own small, comfortable, self-referential mould of being. It was resistant to the outside world and the power of change sweeping by. For this the directors and Fred May must bear a large share of the blame. They were content, happy to keep things the way they had been for years, older men hoping the Sixties would just blow away and we could all get back to the maximum wage, 2-3-5 and would there still be sweet sherry with the post-match tea. The directors were local businessmen who did not seem to want to do much more than own the credential of being a director of the largest sporting enterprise in the town and saw no obligation (or had no ability) to reach beyond traditional budget and investment decisions or to connect with the wider football world at all. They believed that football, and Reading FC, should of itself, in some time-honoured way, be popular and demand support from the town and district. Aspiration without action should suffice to keep them in office and the club alive. They hoped for the best but never planned for anything less in an era of small playing staffs and plentiful injuries. The majority of people I've talked to say it was a happy club and maybe if you were inside the club as a director, an official, a long-standing player or a senior officer of the Supporters' Club it was a friendly, comfortable, good-humoured society. But on the other side of those frosted window panes fronting on to Norfolk Road it did not feel like a warm and welcoming club to young players, match officials, new fans, press men and photographers. How could passers-by on the Tilehurst Road not even know there was a football club just yards below them? Even some young fans never knew you could get into the ground from that side!

The great mystery was the inconsistency of performances on the pitch. Reading could swing from brilliant to awful. Ironically the only consistency was failing to win vital home games and in a couple of seasons two or three more home wins would have made all the difference. No-one could put a finger on a single cause so it was probably a combination of factors. Reading dropped two sorts of vital points – sloppy ones to weak teams that they out-played and tough ones in games that really mattered. Mental alertness, concentration, seeing the game out were crucial aspects in preventing the loss of the former. Being physically up and ready for it and confident of the outcome often determined the latter. In both cases strong leadership on the pitch was necessary. Roy Bentley swapped the captaincy around from Johnny Walker to Colin Meldrum to Dick Spiers and back to Meldrum who was the nearest thing the manager had to a protégé on the pitch. But Meldrum didn't really have the experience or the age to dominate and lead the others though he set a great example by his physical effort. When times were tough Reading did not have enough, or even any, leaders on the pitch. Bentley tended to assess players in terms of capability rather than character, perhaps realising that shortcoming when he belatedly tried to sign Jim Iley. Clubs tend to be more motivated when defending a winning position than chasing one. Reading never had a sufficiently good and sustained start to a league season to have the whole club and support feeling that here was a leading position they must somehow cling onto.

Reading were often excellent when the match mattered more to the other team and thus took down several promotion

161

candidates. But when the match mattered as much to Reading as the opponent, often the case in local derbies, they seemed to lack the mental grit, the fighting spirit and they froze. It's the difference between playing relaxed and tense. The mix of very few natural leaders and being a comfortable, happy band played into a lack of ruthlessness, even bravery, in the very harsh world of the Sixties' Third Division. Away from home Reading's forwards were too often, too quickly battered into submission and gave up. They did not have the physical stature, youth or, in some cases, the basic fitness to compete. When the chips were down, especially in the first half of Bentley's time, Reading were a bit of a soft touch away. But the playing squad was not large enough to allow Bentley to make wholesale, sweeping changes and the budget not large enough to bring in several new men at a time.

Having larger crowds spending more money at Elm Park might have encouraged the board to invest more in the team. But the trend was for the gates to go down, despite a post 1966 World Cup bounce in the country at large. It came to the point where 10,000 would be a good crowd at Reading but a poor one at Swindon. The contemporary reports seethe with the anger, frustration and boredom of supporters, aspects of the Elm Park experience which are largely forgotten by the people I have talked to recently. Yet there is no doubt that the relationship between the club and its supporters was volatile and at times unhealthy. There was a great, latent, desire for football success in the town and county, a reservoir of thousands willing to watch home and away, willing to give Bentley's men another go, or even Wheeler's Reserves, if there was a chance to be joyful and triumphant. But there wasn't a reservoir of patience and goodwill to tide the players, the manager, the club over the harder times. Not only was there the usual lack of a Reading identity or patriotism to draw upon but there was also the sense that the club was not trying its hardest – and rather took its supporters for granted anyway.

162

The club just didn't see that the relationship wasn't there. Every so often the Supporters' Club and the local press would try to formalise some vocal backing for the team but the recurrent disappointments thinned the numbers and the enthusiasm. The club's own acid remarks, sometimes over the loudspeaker, exacerbated the situation. The support wasn't great but there were reasons for that.

Roy Bentley left Reading FC much as he found it in terms of the league table, weaker at the turnstile, stronger in the awareness of its problems. The Board was largely the same, Fred May was still holding the purse-strings, Dick, Rod, Denis and Mike were still in the dressing room getting rubbed down by old Jimmy Wallbanks as they had been when he arrived in 1963. The club was stationary. There were memories of good and / or likeable players and several great performances, notably in the cups. And let's face it Oldham, Brentford and Walsall all spent a lot more money than Reading and got no further. Bristol Rovers, Bournemouth, Shrewsbury and Mansfield were all still in Division Three as well. There was never much fear of relegation to the wilds of Division Four – and Aldershot. Bentley had kept Reading ticking along without moving. It was just that the tick was getting very annoying.

The aftermath

Jack Mansell was the aftermath; the shock treatment for sleepy Reading. In his two and a half years Mansell achieved many things that Roy Bentley did not in his six years: buying lots of players, selling players for £20,000+, getting in loan players, playing football of a quality recognised nationally, getting Reading to the top of Division Three in the spring, having Reading matches featured on TV, playing pre-season friendlies abroad, hiring a PR and marketing guy, being knocked out of the FA Cup by a non-league club, getting relegated to Division Four. Unlike Bentley, Mansell never won a promotion with a Football League club.

His was a gloriously false dawn. At last, for a while it looked like the real thing as Reading swept to the top of the table in late February 1970 playing scintillating football in front of regular home crowds of 15,000 or more. Mansell imposed himself firmly on every aspect of the club. By the end of his first full season *all* of Bentley's players had gone, clean sweep. The last to go was Denis Allen, converted to centre-half to replace his old mucker Dick Spiers. Mansell brought in seven new players at the start of the season and six during it, raising about £90,000 from selling Peter Silvester, George Harris, Colin Meldrum, John Collins and Tom Jenkins (a young winger he'd only just bought). Poised possibly for promotion, but with a leaky and slow defence, Mansell went to the Board once more for a cheap, young defender from Fulham, just £5,000, but the Board for some reason (Mansell was not the most deferential of men) drew the line. The defence shipped 14 goals in the next four games and the season faded away into a Bentley-like 8th place finish, seven points off the promotion places. Like Bentley in 1967-68, Mansell couldn't repeat the successful formula of the previous season. Nevertheless, it was a considerable shock when, after being 8th in the table in early March 1971, form and morale spiralled out of control and

164

Reading ended up relegated on goal average, a disputed own goal being the difference. The shock treatment had killed the Second Division dream, the level where Swindon and Oxford were now contentedly developing their own thing. Reading's derby for the next two seasons (until *they* were promoted!) was down at Aldershot's Rec. Mansell was sacked in October 1971 after a 0-5 defeat at Northampton and 1-8 home defeat for the Reserves. In his 106 League matches Mansell's team conceded four or more goals on 17 occasions and averaged 81 goals against per season. He was a great believer in attacking football.

The opportunity of the Sixties for Reading was to get into the Second Division at a time when interest in football was burgeoning and when rival southern clubs like Swindon, QPR, Ipswich, Bristol City and Crystal Palace (all clubs with similar histories) were making progress up the ladder. This was a genuine opportunity to build the club and its supporter base at a time of expansion and optimism. But it was not taken and, in my view, set the club back about twenty years. As support for the game weakened in the late Seventies and early Eighties Reading weakened further to the point it almost went out of existence in 1983. Between 1971-72 and 1983-84 Reading spent eight seasons in Division Four, gradually getting the hang of how to get promoted from it. First time it took five seasons, then two seasons and finally straight back in one. The club has not seen Division Four football since then. The last of these promotions (1983-84) was achieved by a club quite different in character.

Frank Waller's chairmanship meandered on through the Fourth Division years and when the club was back in the Third it was no better than an under-resourced mid-table outfit. Around Waller there were still familiar faces. In the boardroom was Leslie Davies and Jim Brooks, the former chairman of the Supporters' Club. Gordon Neate was in the groundsman's hut, Maurice Evans came back as assistant manager and then

165

took over as manager in 1977, Dick Spiers was sending in scouting reports, Dougie Webb's wife Joan was working in the office and his son, Neil, was in the youth team then the first team. And when Fred May, at the age of 70, finally put the top on his pen, lo and behold who should be the new secretary in August 1977 but one Roy Bentley. In his time away he tried his hand at bar work, journalism, semi-professional poker and managing Thatcham Town. The family feel Bentley must have sensed on his arrival in 1963 was still there and now he was part of the family, returning, the prodigal ex-manager.

It was unmistakably, and for all Maurice Evans' valiant efforts as manager, a club in advanced, sclerotic decay. It had lost faith with its public to the extent that fewer than 3,000 routinely attended home matches in 1982-83. Waller, coming up to 30 years on the board and having got nowhere, decided it was a lost cause. There were a lot of lost causes in early Thatcher's Britain. He and media mogul chairman of Oxford United Robert Maxwell proposed a merger of the two clubs into an entity called at first Thames Valley Royals and then Thames Valley United. It was an act of business rationalisation that completely misunderstood the nature of football supporting. Both sets of fans were up in arms against the idea. One wonders whether Waller didn't care and had lost all patience or whether he'd simply learned nothing about supporters in 30 years. He had the support of two of his directors and former director Derek Baylis who all agreed to sell their shares to Maxwell. But an organised effort by three rebel directors and the Supporters' Club, an injunction against the use of unsold share capital and an emotional public campaign confounded the plan. Waller and his men finally had to go and it was the end of a very long era.

The new chairman, and effective saviour of the club, was another old name, former player Roger Smee who had made good in the estate agency and property business. He might have been an old name but he was certainly a new broom and

166

swept away the comfortable, old network of Sixties Reading. Out, despite being in the Division Four promotion places at the time, went manager Maurice Evans. Out, because of his sneaky admiration for Maxwell ("despite everything, I rather liked him"), went secretary Roy Bentley. Out went the blue and white hoops again, replaced by various iterations of sky-blue strips. Out went the influence of the Supporters' Club as most of its activities became 'professionalised'. Out went the miasma of lethargy that had enveloped Elm Park for decades. In came rapid promotion from Division Four (1984) and, finally, to Division Two (1986) and a trip to Wembley to win the Simod Cup (1988). It all ended in tears, of course, it always does at this level of football, you've just to learn to enjoy the bits in-between!

John Madejski picked up the pieces in 1990 and gradually put Reading on the football map with a story that's well-known to modern supporters. Two promotions from the third tier (1994 and 2002) and two to the Premier League (2006 and 2012) and the building of a modern stadium on the southern edge of the town (1998). Maurice Evans came back again, sadly all too briefly, as Director of Football in 1999 when Gordon Neate was still the groundsman. Still some threads of the past adorning the new era. But the penurious travails of Alf Smith, Fred May and Roy Bentley belong to a distant age, yet an age hazily recollected by many older supporters.

What hasn't changed?

This will be a shorter answer than what has changed! Football is still the number one sport in the country (it's very rarely referred to as soccer any more). Reading are still the premier sporting and football attraction in Berkshire and still play (since 1992) in blue and white hoops. The town and the club still search for a coherent, distinctive and attractive identity. What happens in the boardroom is still something of a mystery. The passion and vocal backing for the team is still under question. Reading have still never beaten Arsenal.

Looking back over 50 years it is amazing how both football and Reading FC have grown in strength. The doomsayers who claimed the game would die out or the club would fold have been proved manifestly wrong, for the time being at least. As I write Accrington Stanley stand handily placed in the third tier – that was the club that died mid-season in 1962, bringing shame to its town and so much fear to the other lower division clubs. Just one of so many outcomes that no-one could have envisaged in the Sixties. In retrospect the Sixties did not change much for football in general and less still for Reading. There were pop records instead of brass bands before the game and Rod Thornhill grew a moustache. And then it was the Seventies.

Later decline and failure forced reform. Three-up, three down came in 1973-74, three points for a win in 1981-82 and the play-offs in 1986-87. All these measures made the league programme much more exciting. More money in the game made league success more important and the cup competitions were consequently pushed into the shade. The training, control and monitoring of referees have improved immeasurably and certain types of foul play have almost been eradicated. The fitness, dedication and effort of professional footballers is much less questionable than it once was. The stadiums are now comfortable and dry and behaviour within

168

them more closely supervised. No longer do unsupervised bands of nine year-olds roam free. Football, especially at Reading, is now a family affair. It's easier to buy match tickets and they are allocated on a much fairer basis. There is merchandise, marketing and messaging a-plenty. Crowds are bigger and they spend more at the stadium.

In consequence the club has grown in ways that would have Alf Smith and Fred May shaking their heads in disbelief. A multi-million pound training ground, over 200 players in youth development supervised by 25 coaches, a first team squad that has drawn on nearly 50 nationalities of all ethnicities and beliefs, a women's team, recent internationalists for all four of the home nations and many others besides, television coverage of the team's matches accessible all over the world, Swindon and Oxford back in the shade with the Didcot Triangle uncontested for many years, levels of debt a hundred times the amount that frightened Alf Smith, a succession of owners from Russia, Thailand and China and even 'Division Two' status or better for 15 years in a row. Back in the Sixties Alf, Fred, Roy & Co would have been expecting the future to bring men on Mars and Venus, meat and two veg in a big white pill and a monorail replacing the 17 bus up Norcot Road but nothing as fanciful as all this for their club.

What they mastered in their stubborn, unimaginative, proud way was the very unusual feat of making a football club stand virtually still amid the vortex of change and cacophony of complaint all around them. They believed they were keeping the club ticking over but in reality that clock had stopped, unnoticed: not so much the swinging Sixties as the stationary Sixties down Norfolk Road.

It's not moving